Volume 2

Inspiring Next
Innovation Value Chain

Ripi Singh

THIS BOOK SERIES BRINGS
A FEW THINGS FOR EVERYONE,
AND EVERYTHING FOR THE FEW

Research 2016-2018.
Created June 2020.
Expiry June 2025.

Author Royalties go to
COVID-19 Recovery
or Ocean Cleanup.

www.InspiringNext.com/Books

Dedicated

to

My father, Chief Engineer Manmohan Singh,

for

Taking me with him to his workplace every month for
early development of two things he believed to be the most important –
MENTAL MUSCLE and ETHICS.

I was just 10 at that time.

Acknowledgments

When I started my coaching practice with an innovation Framework; the customers, advisors, and well-wishers started asking if my coaching content is available as a book? I wasn't sure if I had sufficient valuable content worthy of a book. Then one day Mr. Vaibhav Garg, an Innovation Manager, and a client, whom I admire for his intellectual insights, said, *"Sir, write a book now. You are ready. Maybe more than 'a' book, since you have so many useful things to share."* Vaibhav stayed by my side providing a critical review of the content throughout the writing and editing process.

Association with the ISO team of innovation experts has been a wonderful learning experience. I am so glad to know Prof. Pierre Deplanche (France), Federico Meneghello (Italy), Prof. Jin Chen (China), James Bromely (U.K.), Magnus Hakvåg (Norway), Irene Makar and Sorin Cohn (Canada), Robin Rowe, Rick Fernandez, and Frank Voehl (USA).

The content of the Inspiring Next series comes from the years of research on innovation and experience working with clients around the world. Some wonderful individuals who put their faith in early versions of the innovation Framework and applied it to their businesses include Dr. Pavan Suri (Singapore), Dr.-Ing Carsten Könke (Germany), Dr. Johannes Vrana (Germany), Prof. Ali Bazzi (Lebanon), Ranvir Singh Rathore (India), Dr. Anukram Mishra (India), Lax Srinivasan (India), Prof. Krishna Pattipati, Dr. Khaled Hassouna, Michael Hoagland, Robert Renz, Bryan Mattimore, Eileen and Matthew Hasson, John Dewey, Chirag Thaker, Jill Meyer, Max Kothari, Mike Racette, Joe Pesticci, Paul Sessions, Brian Kench, Don Locke, Laury DiMarco, Ravi Raghu, Tim Maurer, Rich Dorans, and Michael Rocheleau (all from the USA). Each application helped me get better at innovation coaching and I am very grateful for their engagements and feedback.

Prashant Gupta of Runtime Software (India) worked tirelessly to translate the Framework into a cloud application EinFrame. Candid conversations with Bill McClain encouraged me to write this series. Maya Ramaswamy, a sustainability advocate, covered it all up with her artwork.

Going back to the early years of my coaching practice, few individuals gave me the confidence to keep moving, whenever I was experiencing my lows. Kevin Bouley has always been there to show me hope, connecting me with the right set of individuals, engaging me in intellectually stimulating activities, and showcasing my work to his network. Dr. Pawan Suri and Dr. Rick Pettit never hesitated to help me recalibrate. Rob Berman has been a strong emotional supporter and branding coach.

I attribute the foundations in research and technology management to a decade of learning through United Technologies Leadership Trainings encouraged by Paul Adams, John Zimmerman, and Dan Eigenbrode. Ann Gowdey has been a mentor and coach for almost 15 years, encouraging me to think bigger, helping me transition from an engineer to a manager, to an executive, and then an entrepreneur. Dr. Gopi Katragadda and Dr. G.P. Singh were my former leadership mentors. Late Prof. A.K. Rao, Prof. T.S. Ramamurthy, Prof. B. Dattaguru, Prof. A.R. Ingraffea, Prof. V.S. Malhotra, Prof. S.C. Sharma, and Prof. S.N. Atluri, were my Engineering teachers through the graduate program and early career. Their leadership style still inspires me to do the right thing in the right way, for the organization and the people, no matter what. Often, I just get to an answer by asking *"What would Dattaguru or G.P. do in this situation?"* Just after Coronavirus, I quickly adapted the process G.P. followed soon after 9/11 for his business.

I would like to acknowledge the good that came out of a few naysayers, who triggered me to both improve the models and how I express them.

My lovely wife Anu Kaur and my son AJ Singh, who have both been by my side encouraging me to excel for almost three decades now. Let's not forget all those who are helping us deal with the Coronavirus through innovations in medicine, and service.

– Ripi Singh, June 30, 2020.

Foreword

Having known Ripi Singh for more than 20 years, I am very happy to see this set of 4 volumes by him on innovation. Ripi is well qualified to write this having played the roles of an academician, an industry researcher, an industry research leader, and an innovation coach. Ripi is a deep thinker and an honest technology voice. He is strong on his technology fundamentals and has innovatively applied it in startup ecosystems, industry-university partnerships, as well as in conglomerates.

The topic of innovation has been addressed by several leading lights including Clayton Christenson who died, recently, in January 2020. Ripi's work is still much needed and timely as it covers the most recent concerns of human health and comfort while being inclusive of our dear planet. 2019-2020 has been a year of COVID-19, de-globalization, post-truth politics, student unrest, #metoo impact, US President's impeachment, UK political roller-coaster, and visible climate change impact. These broad trends impact technical directions. COVID-19 has placed a demand for fast health screening and testing, de-globalization has resulted in increased regulations for data sovereignty. Post-truth politics demand technology solutions to detect fake news, images, and videos. Governments have used face-detection technologies to identify persons of interest. Climate change has increased the consciousness of the carbon footprint of the digital age. Given this context, the thesis of Ripi's book, Inspiring Next Purposeful Innovation, is timely and relevant.

Ripi is systematic in covering the topics including the articulation of purpose, connecting it to the markets, using a framework for execution, and leveraging technology for competitiveness. The correlation across purpose, projects, profile, and people is unique. This holistic model covering strategic and tactical practices accounting for mindset is well-positioned to help organizations bring innovation into their culture.

I also appreciate Ripi tying in ISO 56000 to ensure that current thought processes on innovation management are leveraged while bringing in new thinking. Ripi serves as an expert on US team developing these standards which gives him a good vantage point.

Ripi also brings into each chapter, the impact of the recent pandemic on innovation and the need for structured innovation to bounce forward from it. Although the pandemic situation is still evolving and we are all anxious about the next normal, there is useful guidance in here to help leaders prepare for whatever comes next. His book series is practical with the right prompts to capture key take-aways for your work.

I believe that Ripi's book series will add significant value to both organizations beginning their innovation journey as well as those who are well along their way. I wish Ripi the best, and the readers a purposeful innovation journey.

– Gopichand Katragadda, Ph.D.
Founder and CEO at Myelin Foundry
Former Group CTO, Tata Sons
Former MD, GE Technology Center.

The story of how Gopi inspired me to synthesize various tools and practices into the framework is in Volume-3 Chapter-1.

Table of Contents

Important Orientation to the Book Series

OUR INDUSTRY DOES NOT RESPECT TRADITION,
IT ONLY RESPECTS INNOVATION.
— SATYA NADELLA

After a keynote lecture on *Purposeful Innovation* in 2019, a very graceful lady walked up to me, introduced herself as Cleo, the CEO of a services company, and asked, *"Do I need to hire a Chief Innovation Officer?"* My response was, *"Only if you want to grow! ... If you want to wait and watch, a Chief Risk Officer will do; ... and if you are comfortable with the current state, please hire a Chief Prayer Officer!"*

The 4th Industrial Revolution has put innovation at the center stage of discussion across the world since 2015. The technology-driven change has already been fast and furious, coming from all directions. We need an open mind and a suite of processes to develop, adapt, and apply digital technologies that are fusing with the physical reality.

Innovation is the need of the hour. The global pandemic Coronavirus has just pushed everyone out of their comfort zone. Within 6 months of incubation in China, it has infected over 10 million people, killing over 500,000 in over 200 countries. Every country is scrambling to manage the health of the population, while trying to juggle the economic realities from widespread lockdowns. Creativity at home and innovation in the workplace are witnessing enormous opportunities coming out of human survival instincts. It is as if the world has gotten a crash course on crisis innovation. The next three years will be an era for the innovator to bring a new normal to the world, fueled by novel business models, Industry 4.0 technologies, and a social purpose.

Innovation is hard. We perceive it to be hard because of the uncertainty and risk of novel ideas and experimentation. Thinking and attempting something different, with potentially little or no short-term reward, can be emotionally draining. Our natural tendency is to fall back on known methods to arrive at solutions. In most of the work environments, we tag not making mistakes or avoiding an embarrassing failure as outstanding performance. However, this is an unavoidable part of experimentation. In my experience, the biggest barrier to innovation is leadership lacking the courage to go with the minority opinion or weak market signals. The moment we fall into driving the consensus amongst a group of responsible managers, we end up with an average acceptable next step, that everyone can see; at the cost of disengaging the visionaries and their opinions.

Innovation can be made easy. If we could agree on a process where the risk of exploration can be managed, and a mindset where ideas and lessons (failures) are welcome, we can bring innovation into our culture. We can take a portfolio approach where the total output is way more when accounting for some of the failures (learnings), as compared to limited attempts with guaranteed success.

The approach to innovation presented in the first four volumes integrates strategic innovation and tactical execution within a common framework called '+4π' which means looking at the subject from all directions, like 360° in 3-Dimension (3D). Symbol '+' denotes that it is additive. It is based on a core process, from purpose-driven ideation to monetization, which is enhanced by a suite of enabling tools and tips that bring discipline to various aspects of innovation management. The framework asserts that innovation can be much more affordable and accelerated through a disciplined approach, now fully supported by the International Organization of Standards (ISO).

The +4π Framework has evolved from decades of practice in solving tough problems at high-tech companies, several Research and Development (R&D) turnaround assignments, and partnerships with the best of the schools around the world. More recently, engagement with global experts on the subject, while writing ISO 56000 series on Innovation Management, has been a precious exercise in benchmarking and validation of the approach presented in this book series. Throughout the series, I have occasionally shared my current thinking with some raw models, that are still under research, and are unproven. I have disclosed them appropriately with an intent that readers might find an application to experiment and derive value; after all, this is a book on innovation, written to inspire exploration.

How to Extract Best Value from this Book Series?

This book series is all about rebuilding the innovation muscle, which we all had as children, and which we have demonstrated in the face of the recent pandemic. The first four volumes help you address your next need. It could be a search for the next **purpose** (why?), execution of your next **project** (what?), building your next innovation **profile** or **mindset** (how?).

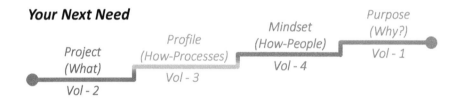

Volume-1 will help you identify your **next purpose** (Why?). Your purpose may be merely to drive or turn your business around financially, or you could push through the 4th Industrial Revolution. At yet another higher level, you may be in pursuit of creating a better social life for human beings, and finally, some of you may be inspired to work on a balance between economic and ecological systems of the planet earth for the sake of humanity. Business leaders must not skip this.

Volume-2 will guide you with steps to your **next project** - product, service, or business model (What?). It systematically walks you through the steps of opportunity identification, ideation, development, risk reduction, in alignment with your purpose. Innovation managers must not skip this.

Volume-3 provides you a framework to build the **next profile** driven by the purpose (Process How?). It provides a set of synergistic tools that will empower you to create a *Strategic Innovation* roadmap, build your *Innovation Capital*, manage *Innovation Value Chain*, and keep it *Efficient*. The objective is to get you ahead of the competition. Innovation leaders must not skip this.

Volume-4 provides you with tricks to build the **next mindset** (People How?) and is important, since processes and tools are not sufficient to become a consistent innovator. Leaders and managers tasked to bring change to the organization must not skip this.

Each volume carries a summary of other volumes in the form of a chapter. This helps with a recap or a broader perspective when you skip the details.

If you already have a well-functioning innovation engine, you can treat this series as a tool chest, where you can pick the tool you need and just use it. Some are simple to use, some power tools need external energy, and some delicate ones may even need surgical precision. Many of the tools are multi-purpose and adaptable. At times, you may find some that serve opposite functions, just like your tool chest has cutting tools as well as bonding tools. Please do not view them as confounding, as each tool may just offer another way of accomplishing something different, that you may need some other time.

If you wish to start or accelerate your innovation journey, you can use this book series to align your entire organization with purposeful innovation. You can implement processes to consistently innovate, build the innovation mindset, and grow sustainably. The processes, tools, models, and tricks are sequenced to progressively build an awareness and appreciation of innovation, and the concepts within the framework will serve you best while reading like a typical book bundle from front of Volume-1 to back of Volume-4. All chapters and volumes provide an opportunity for introspection or self-assessment.

> Each chapter closes with a *Selfie Moment* section.
> Each volume closes with a *Time to Reflect* chapter.
> Volume-4 closes with a *Time to Liberate* chapter.

These sections and chapters have been specifically placed to help you plan your journey towards a more innovative organization. Change agents must read all four volumes and work through the selfie moments and introspection exercises with the eye of the company, and then create a plan using the last chapter of Volume-4. During execution you can reference any of the volumes like handbooks - go to any chapter/section and use that as a stand-alone tool, process, guide, or even just cite a story or share a quote.

Please appreciate that innovation capability development is a long and hard journey to build the mental muscle. Just like building the physical muscle requires regular visits to the gym, proteins for months, adequate rest, and a coach; The mental muscle requires discipline, consistency, commitment, patience, and coaching. Once you are on your way, please give this muscle enough time and energy to develop.

ISO is providing Innovation Management Guidance (ISO 56000) as a series of standards. This book series would be incomplete without an introductory mention to various standards at appropriate places in the series. The ISO standards are copyright and available for purchase. In this book series, the mention is kept to a minimum, mostly from the public sections of the official ISO website. I have used a few definitions from the officially released versions, with an intent to promote the use of the ISO standards, through demonstration of relevance and value. If you wish to apply the ISO standards, please purchase them from www.iso.org.

The unedited content from ISO is specifically highlighted in this style.

ISO 56000 provides key insights to establish an innovation system and does not contain any requirement. The guidance is generic and applicable to all types of organizations. While on one hand, ISO provides flexibility to adapt, it is also subject to interpretation and requires tools and models for successful conformance. The $+4\pi$ Framework in this series of books provides the necessary tools for such conformance.

Pandemic as a dislocation. Just when I was finishing this book series, the world was taken over by Coronavirus, and life came to a standstill, awaiting a new normal. We can address it as a dislocation, having disrupted every sector, industrial domain, country, and society. Since this has ushered an era of the innovator, I was suddenly compelled to add a chapter addressing a tough time scenario to each volume and inspired to plan Volume-5 as a follow-through.

Volumes on Industry-specific applications will follow.

With due respect to so many experts on the subject of innovation and strategy around the world, I make a sincere effort to give them credit through references and even through using some of their original language without distortion; I do not intend this to violate any copyrights, but I mean it as a prior art or research plugged into various models in the $+4\pi$ Framework for purposeful innovation.

Disclaimer: My personal anecdotes at the start of each chapter, providing context to the topic, are based on actual life stories, slightly altered to protect individual and company identity.

> ### Failure to Explore and Learn is Not an Option

Snapshot of Volume-2

This is the second Volume in the series. It begins with a summary of Volume-1 and ends with summaries of Volumes-3 and Volume-4 as the last two chapters. The overall content of the four volumes and the contents of this volume are graphically shown here.

Series Content
Next Purpose *(Why)*
- The Innovation
- The Purpose
- Financial Drive
- Technology Push
- Social Pull
- Sustainable Development
- Purpose in a Tough Time

Next Project *(What)*
- Innovation Value Chain
- Deep Market Insight
- Structured Ideation
- Purposeful Qualification
- Creative Execution
- Variations in Value Chain
- Value Chain in a Tough Time

Next Profile *(How-Process)*
- Innovation Framework
- Innovation Strategy
- Innovation Capital
- Innovative Activity
- Lean Innovation
- Framework in a Tough Time

Next Mindset *(How-People)*
- Innovation Struggle
- Unshackle the Past
- Reboot Leadership
- Re-Ignite Creativity
- Embrace Exploration
- Mindset in a Tough Time

Time to Liberate
- Define the Future State
- Start the Journey
Appendices

Volume-2 Content
Innovation Value Chain

Orientation to the Series

V1. Innovation Purpose

1. Innovation Value Chain
2. Deep Market Insight
3. Structured Ideation
4. Purposeful Qualification
5. Creative Execution
6. Variations in Value Chain
7. Value Chain in a Tough Time
8. Time to Reflect

V3. Innovation Framework

V4. Innovation Mindset

Appendices

Recap[1] of Volume-1
Inspiring Next Innovation Purpose

INNOVATION DISTINGUISHES BETWEEN A LEADER AND A FOLLOWER
– STEVE JOBS

In 1978, growing up in a village in India, one day I learned that someone in the neighborhood has purchased a radio that also shows a movie picture. My curiosity pushed me to learn more, and I had my first look at this big box, we later learned was called television. My father explained the terms invention, scientist, and inventor; and I realized that is what I want to be. He got me 'Meccano' - a model construction system to build creative toys by putting pieces together. For many years, I was a living room (re)inventor assembling working models of earthmoving machinery. Today, we use the term *innovation*. 40 years later, I believe I understand what it entails, even though I can't define it precisely or uniquely.

Different experts have different perspectives on what innovation is and what it is not. Some of my fellow experts say that innovation is a process, others call it a skill or a competency. I think it is **a mindset** that inspires you to challenge assumptions and break away from the generally accepted norms. A mindset that explores new options, experiments and learns from failures, and eventually creates a new value for someone, be it a single user or entire humanity.

There are several definitions of Innovation. In Volume-1, I shared a few of them to provide a perspective that I believe to be relatively simple to

---

[1] You may skip it, if you have good recollection of Volume-1.

comprehend and apply. I like the one compiled by Crossan and Apaydin[2] in 2010:

> *Innovation is:*
> *production or adoption, assimilation, and exploitation of*
> *a value-added novelty in economic and social spheres;*
> *renewal and enlargement of products, services, and markets;*
> *development of new methods of production; and*
> *establishment of new management systems.*
> *It is both a process and an outcome.*

This definition is the most comprehensive, as it captures several important aspects of innovation: it includes both internally conceived and externally adopted innovation (production or adoption); it highlights innovation as more than a creative process, by including application (exploitation); it emphasizes intended benefits (value-added) at one or more levels of analyses; it leaves open the possibility that innovation may refer to a relative, as opposed to the absolute, novelty of an innovation; and it draws attention to the two roles of innovation (a process and an outcome), the keyword being *'outcome'*.

ISO has recently converged on a simple set of terms and descriptors[3]. Accordingly,

‖ *Innovation is 'New or changed entity, realizing or redistributing value.'*

New or changed entity corresponds to a new or improved product or process, or a combination thereof, that differs significantly from previous products or processes. Realizing or redistributing value indicates that it has been made available to potential users or brought into use.

In this context, the concept of innovation is characterized by novelty and value. To realize value, the entity must be introduced, implemented,

---

[2] A Multidimensional Framework of Organizational Innovation: A Systematic Review of the Literature; M M Crossan and M Apaydin; J of Mgmt Stu; Vol 47, pp 1154; 2010.
[3] ISO 56000:2020 – Fundamentals and Vocabulary; Feb 2020.

deployed, adopted, or used to a certain extent. Thus, novelty and value are both necessary and sufficient characteristics of the concept of innovation. This also means that insights, ideas, and inventions without the manifestation of **value**, are not innovations.

Learning to innovate is like learning to paint or play a piano. There is both logic and art to it. You can pick up the logic in a day, but the mind-memory-muscle coordination takes months or practice. It can be learned. It is not the privilege of just the gifted few.

Innovation Classification based on Scope

From 30,000 feet, I view the realization of value at different levels: from individual, organizational, to societal.

- Workbench Innovation for personal efficiency/ effectiveness.
- Process Innovation for bottom line.
- Business Model Innovation for market recapture.
- Product and Service Innovations for top line.

Innovation Classification based on Value Creation (Attribute)

Once again, the innovation may create different levels of value, at a different pace, under varied scenarios of collaboration and budgetary constraints. Let us define a few, that we will discuss later in this book at much greater lengths.

- Evolutionary Innovation (Small improvement).
- Eco-adaptive Innovation (Translation).
- Peripheral Innovation (Adjacent).
- Crisis Innovation (Emergency).
- Burst Innovation (Rapid).
- Bold Innovation (Multi-faceted and integrated).
- Frugal Innovation (Resource starved).
- Open Innovation (External participation).
- Classified Innovation (Secrecy).
- Breakthrough Innovation (Significantly new).

- Disruptive Innovation (Turning point).
- Responsible Innovation (Socially conscious).
- Open-source Innovation (Social and free).
- Dark Innovation (Damaging).

Volume-1 Chapter-1 defined these in details.

Innovator Classification

All the above classifications are based on attributes of actions or outcomes. They have not yet addressed the two frequently asked questions:

1. Is there a yardstick to assess how innovative is your company?
2. Is there a systematic way of becoming more innovative?

Here is my proposal for the classification of an organization using a profile from a market perspective.

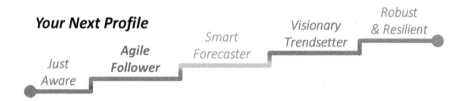

Just Aware

These are the companies that have successfully innovated and **know how** to. They continuously struggle to sustain it and keep losing to the competition. Often, the primary reason for being so is overly inflated self-worth from being innovative 'once upon a time' and not being able to develop enough of an outward perspective. Kodak, Blackberry, and Blockbuster are well-known examples. During one of my keynote talks, the audience loved the closing remark, *"Netflix'it or get Blockbusted!"*

Agile Follower

These companies innovate profitably in **response to market demand** and successfully compete on cost and time to market. They are listening to the customers, benchmarking themselves against the competition, and but continuously working hard to compete directly. Typically, they are good at '*How*' and are actively listening to the customer for '*What*'. The majority of companies fall into this category.

Smart Forecaster

These companies consistently innovate in **anticipation of market demand** and try to be amongst the first few in the marketplace to easily recover their investment. They empathize with the customer to understand the unarticulated needs, invest in competitive intelligence to predict their moves, and compete on offering continuously increasing value ahead of the competition. They typically understand the '*What*' and the '*How*' and are seeking '*Why*'. Examples include Airbus, Ford, Sony, and other such companies.

Visionary Trendsetter

These companies are natural at innovation and **create a demand** with new products and services. They educate the customers on '*Why and How*' of their offerings, while making the competition irrelevant. They start with '*A Why Not*'. SpaceX, Lockheed Martin, Cox, Pepsi, Tesla, are some examples.

Robust and Resilient

These companies consistently deliver profitable innovation in the face of uncertainty; they are the trendsetters, who have also built so much branding, talent, and cash reserves that they can absorb any emerging disruption, even when sometimes missing a trendsetting scenario. They have developed **some degree of immunity** to market forces. These are Google, Apple, Amazon, … class.

Why not start with a Why Not?

This simplistic Innovation Profile definition will be used throughout the book series, and it will help you orient and think through your journey. They represent specific characteristics which will be discussed at length in Vol-3. I urge you to self-assess where you are today and where would you like to be, to get full value. This is a good starting point for any innovation journey.

Just a note of caution, not everyone needs to be a *Visionary Trendsetter*. There is nothing wrong in being a *Smart Forecaster*. In fact, the *Forecaster* profile offers stability and growth at an affordable risk. Being a *Trendsetter* entails a lot of risk, and is not for everyone, or every occasion.

Innovation Purpose

In the business world, startups are invariably innovative, emerging out of an entrepreneur's purpose or passion. They scale up into a business with formal structure; which then slides into the abyss of financial objectives. Unfortunately, the purpose now gets buried under some 'mission statement' that very few employees understand. Most of the employees frequently walk past the mission statement on the wall to address their boss or customer's immediate need. Innovation becomes an enabling tool with emphasis on speed and cost. The larger the organization, the deeper this abyss gets.

Then comes the annual cycle of revising the business strategy; supposed to guide the teams on how to compete successfully in the marketplace. New products, services, or new markets is one of those guidelines. Innovation and strategy are often mistakenly viewed as separate approaches, and I hear CEO's saying "*let's get our strategy first, and then we will work on innovation.*" That is as good a sign of an aging organization as any.

Purposeful Innovation is the best strategy.

It is not a keyword or an action item to support strategy. Purposeful innovation is the way for an organization to be forward-looking and deliver true lasting value, besides financial responsibility and sustainability. Ray Stasieczko says, *"Innovative organizations understand the importance of relevant products; while dying organization stay obsessed with selling the relevancy of their soon to be obsolete products."* Innovation is the most important factor in economic viability, technology adaption, social well-being, and sustainable development.

The purpose generally comes from the heart of the leadership, and it can be at various levels, broadly classified below:

Volume-1 Chapter-2 presented this hierarchy of purpose model.

Financial Drive

Where the purpose is to provide enough sales and profit margins, to stay in business, and perhaps grow. I find this to be the lowest level of purpose, although mostly described, justified, and referred to under the context of *Business decisions*. I would prefer to call it merely an objective so you can exist for a larger purpose, … to create value in some form.

Management in the 20th century was, in large part, the art of strategic planning. You gathered information about markets, competitors, and other trends and then planned accordingly. Strategy was like a game of chess. You planned each move in response to a changing board and anticipation of competitors' moves. Primary tools include Voice of the Customer (VOC), Strength, Weakness, Opportunities, and Threats (SWOT), Continuous Product Improvement, and Business Model Innovation.

Today, the technology cycles move faster than planning cycles ever could, so we need to take a more Bayesian approach to strategy. Instead of trying to get every move right — which is impossible in today's environment — we need to try to become less wrong over time. Essentially, we need to treat strategy like a role-playing game, taking quests that earn us experience and artifacts along the way.

That means, we will need to plan differently. In addition to strategic planning, or planning based on things we know or we think we know, we need to start innovation planning or planning based on things we need to learn to solve new and important problems.

> Today, you may plan the journey as much as you like,
> but
> you must prepare for unanticipated diversions.

A significant question in this age of rapid innovation is *"What will Make Your Business Irrelevant in 5 Years?"* Hint: Market forces, technology, talent, business model, or these big four (Amazon, Google, Apple, Elon Musk) endeavors that have emerged from zero to the top in about 25 years; half a career span for most of us these days.

You don't plan the journey as much as you prepare for it. I would prefer to use the terms *'Strategic Readiness'* over *'Strategic Planning.'*

Volume-1 Chapter-3 covered purposeful innovation for Financially Driven companies.

Technology Push – Industry 4.0 [4]

When the purpose is to successfully develop, leverage, enable, exploit the cyber-physical integration into process, product, service, or business application. It is OK to have a technology development as a defined purpose, but it makes a lot more sense to connect it with an impact on everyday living.

---

[4] https://www.plattform-i40.de/I40/Navigation/EN/Home/home.html

The original portfolio of technologies within Industry 4.0 had Big Data and Analytics, Autonomous Robots, Simulation, Horizontal and Vertical System Integration, Industrial Internet of Things, Cybersecurity, Cloud, Additive Manufacturing, and Augmented Reality. Now it should also include Artificial Intelligence (AI), Blockchain, Voice Control and Assistance, Quantum Computers, and 5G. Digital Twin and Digital Thread which connect the cyber and physical spaces are the key to creating value through relevant applications.

Industry 4.0 offers huge opportunities at various levels from cleaning the oceans down to desktop effectiveness or point of action. Different profiles look at technology differently.

Agile Followers watch & adapt as and when they see maturity and value.
Smart Forecasters are a little ahead of the game adapting, tweaking, & leveraging these to create new products and services.
Visionary Trendsetters develop these technologies, and demonstrate the value through application.

Interestingly, the companies with a financial purpose frown upon these technology projects as a cost driver. While those with social or sustainability purposes like to leverage these technologies as tools. Industry 4.0 is scary or cute to those who are still working to discover their purpose.

Technology for the sake of technology could be a purpose for the techies; however, the leaders ought to think of making life a little better for humans, across all domains of everyday living – home, city, work, manufacturing, healthcare, mobility, … towards the next revolution …

Volume-1 Chapter-4 covered purposeful innovation for the 4th industrial revolution.

Social Pull – Society 5.0 [5]

When the purpose is to create a better life for human beings. This is the Japanese perspective and response to Germany's Industry 4.0; Cyber-Physical-Human confluence to create a smart society. This is the onset of purposeful innovation and it now makes sense. Technology for the sake of technology or money only brings us halfway. Application for the benefit of humanity is where it ought to lead us.

Portfolio of leading social pulls include smart living (homes and city), smart healthcare (eHealth, mHealth, wearables, ambient assisted living), smart mobility (indoor, outdoor, intra-city, inter-city, cross-continent), smart grid and renewables (substations, mobile, meters, appliance) and smart workplace (factory, office).

Society 5.0 is an attempt to create a human-centered society that balances economic advancement with the resolution of social problems by a system that highly integrates cyberspace and physical space. Social reform (innovation) in Society 5.0 will achieve a forward-looking society that breaks down the existing sense of stagnation, a society whose members have mutual respect, transcending the generations, and a society in which everybody can lead an active and enjoyable life. All of the technologies in industry 4.0 and supporting business models have the potential for social transformation.

Volume-1 Chapter-5 covered purposeful innovation for the 5th social revolution.

> Eventually, if everything around you is *smart*,
> would you still need another purpose? Of course.

---

[5] https://www8.cao.go.jp/cstp/english/society5_0/index.html

Sustainable Development[6]

This is where your purpose goes beyond humanity and addresses the sustainability of life on our planet for a long time to come. True sustainability[7] requires a balance of economic, social, and environmental factors in equal harmony. Sustainable development is defined as *'Development that meets the needs of the present without compromising the ability of future generations to meet their own needs.'*

United Nations (UN) document called Brundtland Report[8] provided early guidance on the subject in 1987. **Humanity has the ability to make development sustainable.** The concept of sustainable development does imply limits - not absolute limits but limitations imposed by the present state of technology and social organization on environmental resources and by the ability of the biosphere to absorb the effects of human activities. This understanding and evolution continued with eight 'Millennium Development Goals' for the period 2000-2015 and now a set of 17 Sustainable Development Goals for the period 2015-2030. These 17 goals are somewhat hierarchical. The first few are basic and more relevant to the developing countries. The ecological and spiritual goals are more relevant for the developed countries at this time.

Progress is being made in many places, but, overall, action to meet the Goals is not yet advancing at the speed or scale required. The Decade of Action 2020-2030 calls for accelerating sustainable solutions to all the world's biggest challenges – ranging from poverty and gender to climate change, inequality, and closing the finance gap.

---

[6] https://sustainabledevelopment.un.org
[7] What is Sustainability and What is Sustainable Development? May 2020;
https://circularecology.com/sustainability-and-sustainable-development.html.
[8] Our Common Future; Report of the World Commission on Environment and Development: Brundtland Report; https://sustainabledevelopment.un.org/content/documents/5987our-common-future.pdf; UN 1987.

Earth Overshoot Day: Experts at the Global Footprint Network are monitoring the world's ecological footprint each year and pinpointing the day that we have officially demanded more from nature than what the Earth can regenerate. This day is referred to as Earth Overshoot Day[9]. It is computed by dividing the planet's biocapacity (the amount of ecological resources Earth can generate that year), by humanity's Ecological Footprint (humanity's demand for that year).

The planet's capacity to sustain resource use and waste production was breached in 1970. And it has been sliding in the wrong direction ever since. The only periods of rollback or positive movement have been during the three recessions: 1981-82, 1990-91, and 2007-09; and perhaps 2020 due to the Coronavirus Pandemic. We will know that date in early 2021. In 2019, It fell on July 29, which means humanity consumed 1.7 times what Earth gave us. Another interesting perspective is that the prosperous countries have much more impact on Earth Overshoot Day. For the USA as a country, it was March 15, 2019. Imagine, if your budget = 4.9 x sales, and you are forced to use your reserves because your annual revenues only lasted for the first 2.5 months!

An easy inference is when the economy is good, we consume the planet more. So, the **industrial revolution**s, which are giving **society** a false sense of happiness, have certainly led to an adverse impact on our **planet's** ecological balance. It is time to strike a balance between economic and ecological systems.

The number #1 challenge is that the goals are too big and daunting. Each one of us can easily convince ourselves that we cannot make a difference. It is for government bodies, large corporations and philanthropists to save the planet. Well, not really, it ought to be everybody's job. Policies help implement actions that are otherwise not easily adopted – but these policies do not come about without collective input. Each of us, individually, through our needs, wishes and demands convey a message of what is

---

[9] This section is from https://www.footprintnetwork.org/ and https://www.overshootday.org/.

acceptable to consume and produce. Corporate innovators capture the message via surveys, focus groups and demand analysis to decide where to invest and what products to bring to society. Products are a social pull. We should do our share and also educate everyone around us with messaging that is tangible and personal. We should do our share and also educate everyone around us.

Even in the corporate sector the sentiment is slowly changing. Major investment firms are integrating sustainability issues into their investing criteria. Business Roundtable released a new statement in 2019 on the Purpose of a Corporation signed by 181 CEOs who commit to lead their companies for the benefit of all stakeholders: customers, employees, suppliers, communities, and shareholders. One of the five commitments is to protect the environment by embracing **sustainable practices** across the business.

Volume-1 Chapter-6 covered purposeful innovation for sustainability and sustainable development.

Purpose in a Tough Time

At the time of finalizing this book, we entered a pandemic from Coronavirus or COVID-19. That hardship is very revealing of our individual and business purpose. We can see financially driven entities taking advantage of the situation. Technology-driven teams addressing the shortage of hand sanitizer, masks, ventilators, and ripple effects. Socially driven individuals, first responders, health care, and mental healers stepping up to stitch the social fabric. So many individuals and businesses have stepped up to accommodate the needs of society. Many have temporarily shifted their purpose for social good. Although sustainability is not on the human mind, there is a favorable impact from the economic slowdown.

> While the tough times test your resolve to stick to your purpose,
> the purpose also provides emotional strength required to ride
> through a tough time. It may even be revealed, redefined
> temporarily, or even permanently altered.

If you have to resort to financial security in the short term, it is OK, but remember sustainability is best served when you step up your purpose to social good. Your customers and network will remember all those who were around for them during the tough time.

The current pandemic has shed some light on climate control. The favorable ecological impact is an eye-opener in terms of how quickly the life form can come back to occupy space that humans had taken over. The reduced pollution from curtailed driving, flying, and factory shutdown is a grim reminder of what humans should restrain from.

I submit that the purposeful innovation is the right way to go. The purpose around sustainable planet and smart society, through a balanced use of technology should be at the core of every business, community activity, and personal actions.

Volume-1 Chapter-7 covered purposeful innovation in a tough time.

Some Examples

Amazon Mission – To build a place where people can come to find and discover anything, they might want to buy online. Lead with 3 core ideas – lots of choice, fast delivery, and competitive pricing.

Apple Purpose – To empower creative exploration and self-expression

Apple Mission – To bring the best user experience to its customers through its innovative hardware, software, and services.

David Packard's speech to Hewlett Packard in 1960 – Purpose is like a guiding star on the horizon – forever pursued but never reached. Yet although purpose itself does not change; it does inspire change. The very fact that the purpose cannot be fully realized means that an organization can never stop stimulating change and progress.

Google Mission – Organize the world's information and make it universally accessible & useful.

Tesla Mission – Accelerating the world's transition to sustainable ~~transport~~ energy.

Volvo Purpose – An Automobile is driven by people. Safety <u>is and must be</u> the basic principle in all design work. – Cofounders in 1939.

Let's Summarize

In the fast-changing world, the best way to stay relevant is to have a purposeful business. It helps continuously re-align value proposition because the focus is not on tasks, projects, initiatives, or fiscal objectives. It is a lot easier and more palatable to digest the failure of an effort when the eye is on a bigger goal.

> I very much expect purpose-driven companies to have a higher survival rate through the pandemic.

Purpose helps redefine the playing field, because it assumes a lot less, has fewer boundaries, and opens the mind. When I was working on simulating structural failures, I had a certain market opportunity in my field of view. The day I redefined my purpose to be *aviation safety* it turned out to be 100 times bigger; and I ventured into risk-based inspection, life cycle management, human factors; all with structural simulation as the centerpiece. That is the power of the purpose.

The traditional view of the mission statement is to align the organization in terms of priorities and focus, creating efficiency and effectiveness, engaging employees, and retaining customers. That is not enough. When you upgrade your thinking from mission to purpose, you also upgrade alignment to trust in relationships with employees and customers.

Leaders and companies that have effectively defined corporate purpose typically have done so with one of two approaches[10]: retrospective or prospective. The retrospective approach builds on a firm's existing reason for being. It requires that you look back, codify organizational and cultural DNA, and make sense of the firm's past. The focus of the discovery process is internal. In the prospective approach, you look ahead and ask what do you wish to accomplish and impact in the future. I do not expect you to rewrite your purpose in terms of planet sustainability. But I do sincerely hope that whatever innovation purpose you may choose to pursue next, you are at least aware of its impact on sustainability; and you will do the right thing for the planet earth.

If you had already identified next technology (Industry 4.0) or next smart thing (Society 5.0) as a purpose, you might be able to see those in light of moving the date, or refine that so you are working towards a more meaningful purpose.

In other words, you will choose to pursue Responsible Innovation.

---

[10] Put Purpose at the Core of Your Strategy; T W MalnightIvy, I Buche, and C Dhanaraj; https://hbr.org/2019/09/put-purpose-at-the-core-of-your-strategy; HBR, Sept-Oct 2019.

Let's Take a Selfie

Our organization innovation profile is

☐ Aware – Know-how to innovate.
☐   In between.
☐ Agile Follower – Innovating in response to market demand.
☐   In between.
☐ Smart Forecaster – Innovating in anticipation of market demand.
☐   In between.
☐ Visionary Trendsetter – Innovating and creating market demand.
☐   In between.
☐ Robust & Resilient – We got the world under control.

The purpose of my business is at this level

☐ I still cannot wrap my head around this.
☐ Financial growth, one way or the other, Legally and Ethically.
☐ Technology push, whatever can find market acceptance.
☐ Technology push to improve the quality of human life.
☐ Bring people together to make good things happen for society.
☐ Technology push to support UN Sustainable Development Goals
☐ … add your own
☐

I can see an opportunity and a threat to my business from the following technologies

☐ Internet of Things.
☐ Artificial Intelligence.
☐ Robotics and Automation.
☐ Additive Manufacturing (3D Printing).
☐ Augmented Reality.
☐ Competitors who start using these before I can understand them.
☐ … add your own
☐

I can see a social opportunity in the following industries and applications:

☐ Smart living (Home, City, Mobility, etc.).
☐ Better healthcare and hospitality services.
☐ Advanced learning and education.
☐ Smart manufacturing and exotic materials.
☐ Better environment (Air, Water, etc.).
☐ Better animal life (on land, in water).
☐ … add your own.
☐

I am willing to bring others along with me, in my pursuit of a purpose

☐ Train, support, and reward my employees to support our purpose.
☐ Products, processes, and business models, to promote our purpose.
☐ Educate and set expectations with suppliers who understand our purpose.
☐ Recognize and extra support to customers who appreciate our purpose.
☐ Educate regulatory bodies that seek our counsel.
☐ Include promotors, influencer, and sponsors.
☐ … add your own
☐

My Purpose (Statement)

Purpose Validation: Keep iterating the above statement until the answer to all of the following questions is Yes.

☐ Is it compelling enough to make me change my vacation plans?
☐ Is there anything similar that I enjoyed during my school and college?
☐ If I do not do this by the age of 60, will I regret it?
☐ Is this the most important thing to me other than my family and health?
☐ Do I have the competency and personality to successfully pursue it?

My Purpose-Profile Journey looks like

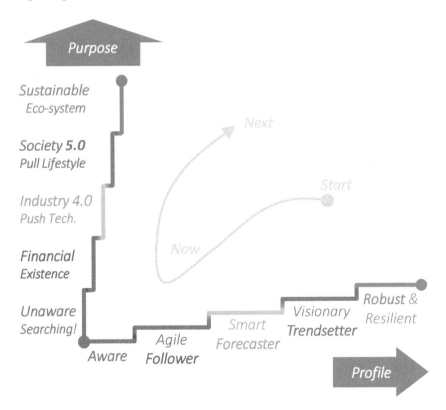

Can you plot your journey on this chart? The light gray is a very typical journey that I come across, and is deliberately kept very light to allow you to draw your line in this chart.

1. Innovation Value Chain

INNOVATION IS THE PROCESS OF TURNING IDEAS INTO
MANUFACTURABLE AND MARKETABLE FORM
— WATTS HUMPREY

With a team of aerospace graduate students in 1995, we took on a challenge to build a *Flying Tiffin* – a box to carry food across the university campus. Today, we would call it a pizza-drone, which was not a popular term back then in India. We sketched around a dozen helicopter type configurations, picked an attractive one, did our preliminary design, and started our search for a financial sponsor. Once, we realized that we may not get all the funding we need, we started brainstorming on what parts can we afford and how. Luckily, we managed to excite a local two-wheeler manufacturer, TVS Motor Company, to offer us a used 4.5HP engine free of cost; though prohibitively heavy for any flight vehicle. That brought us back to the drawing board for resizing around the only engine we had. The helicopter became heavier, larger, at the cost of food box becoming smaller. Taneja Aerospace, an upcoming manufacturer, offered us a small amount of money to build the airframe in exchange for our service to create and host their website – a big deal at that time and place. We then cannibalized a control system from an old materials test lab equipment sitting unused with a friend, and resolved the last of our financial concerns. The shape and size of the control system, took out any remaining room and weight margin for the food box. We could see a flying machine in our future with no payload capacity to carry anything. Another round of iteration and we gave up the look and feel of the machine to at least have enough room for a sandwich. The team went over a dozen learning iterations, and were still excited to follow through, but they ran out of time. The academic semester was over and the students graduated. The following year, another batch of students picked up the engine, the controls, redesigned the airframe for a better look and feel, and with larger payload capacity; a result of a fresh set of minds and eyes. Just before they graduated, they rolled out a fine-looking helicopter from the local hangar (workshop) to an exciting celebration, knowing very well that the rotors were not balanced to the level required for a safe flight. That machine never flew; but the project served the purpose – *taught two batches of graduate students as to what innovation entails.* We also realized the power of network capital that enabled us to get an engine, controls and financial sponsorship.

Simplified Innovation Value Chain

The Innovation Value Chain is a series of connected steps, which lead to an innovative product, service, or a business model. Successful outcomes typically require an innovator to make some assumptions at each step, validate or challenge them at the next step, go back and revise those assumptions if required, continuously build upon new learnings, and iteratively close in on the purpose.

In its simplest form, an innovation is about the visualization of the end solution for a customer, starting with a lot of ideas or opportunities; filtering them down to a few qualified projects; and then ethically executing them to a successful delivery, or, sometimes, to a new learning (failure).

The beginning of an innovation process is always very hazy. It is generally an accidental or deliberate match between an idea and the problem it can solve. It is often difficult to discern whether the idea or the problem came first. Generally, individuals and startups get an idea and start exploring the market opportunity, while corporate innovations search for ideas to go after a market opportunity. In either case, almost everyone goes through several iterative cycles before converging on an idea-market combination worthy of pursuit.

Your Next Project Step

| Market Place Insight | Ideation | Concept Qualification | Execution |

Purpose and Ethics Filters

Value Chain as a Multilayer Filter

The multi-step activity from market insight to market capture is like a multilayer filter. At each step, you remove the options that may not work. From experience, we all know that only a handful of ideas will qualify for execution out of the 100s that are captured. At this stage, you could either create a portfolio of projects, or use a criterion for prioritization.

Marketing folks might see this process as a funnel. But a funnel is a poor metaphor because it allows everything that gets in from the top to get out at the bottom. I prefer to call it a filter. In a well-designed filter, only the desired material comes out at the other end. In the case of the Innovation Value Chain, the filter design is the innovation management process and the human mindset.

Let's briefly understand these steps now, and details in chapters later.

Market Insight

When the objective is to take a new product or a service to the market, you need a good insight into what opportunities exist out there and what you are competing against. This marketplace insight is an absolute necessity to fulfill the desire or purpose to influence it.

Customer insight: The first major step in structured innovation is to define a problem worth solving. The opportunities are all around us, in every little action starting with waking up and having coffee to flying across the world for business or pleasure. We see, hear, use, or talk about new products

3

from toothbrushes to Space Station almost every day. Often, they appear obvious and simple in hindsight, and yet we had never asked for it or thought about it, staying busy doing the same thing, the same way, in our habitual routines.

Competitive insight: Another step is to see what already exists or is in the works to solve the problem you have identified. Once again, there is generally some competition, or an incumbent solution resisting change. And, when you make something new and promising, it invites new competitors to the market.

Chapter-2 will cover details on how various innovation profiles capture and use marketplace insight.

Structured Ideation

This is the most creative and elusive step of the innovation, and generally the origin of the myth that innovation can't be taught, or that innovators are born, not made. Ideation may not be science, but it is certainly not magic. It is probably an art, and sustained practice gets you to a state of mind that is continuously generating great ideas. Experience has shown that the ideas are not a random occurrence, but rather triggered by some form of an intellectual stimulus. This implies that we can create a stimulating environment or devise an exercise to generate hundreds of ideas. Quite often, an ideation session can lead to tapping new markets, in addition to serving a specific pre-defined objective.

Structured Ideation helps in asking the right questions, bringing together perspectives and strengths of the participating members to take steps beyond the obvious solutions and therefore, increasing the innovation potential of a solution, through volume and variety. The structure includes planning, facilitation, technique, triggers, data capture, and preliminary sorting or clustering into themes.

Chapter-3 will briefly discuss a few ideation techniques that are way more effective than traditional brainstorming.

Purposeful Qualification

After a couple of iterations between customer problem and solution ideas, you will get to the stage of assessment of their worth. At this point, you must ask these three questions before investing resources into the ideas.

Value Proposition: Does it add value to a customer/user/consumer? A good value proposition acts as a pain reliever and/or gain creator for a job to be done by a prospective customer.

Purpose & Ethics Check: Does it fit your self-defined purpose and self-imposed ethical standards, in addition to being legally compliant?

Concept Qualification: Can you deliver it profitably, to sustain or grow your own business? Is it dependable, scalable, sustainable, and whatever else it needs to be to align with your purpose in the short or the long run?

I am not offended when people use the traditional term – *Business Case*; I just do not like it, from the perspective of a mindset. A business case generally tends to diminish the purpose down to merely a Financial Drive.

Chapter-4 covers these steps in reasonable detail to make them useable.

Creative Execution

A concept, once qualified needs to be converted into reality. Most companies have some form of project management, or phase-gate process to continuously reduce the execution and market risks. Depending on how much your innovation pushes the envelope of existing knowledge and experience, you need to be prepared to iterate on the value proposition and execution options. The ability to learn and adapt is the key to successful innovation.

Chapter-5 provides detailed steps on defining the innovation project, success criteria, teaming, and the review structure for continuous risk reduction.

ISO 56002 - Innovation Management System - Guidance[11]

ISO 56002:2019 lays out a very similar baseline innovation process that can be configured to suit any initiative.

> *General (Clause 8.3.1) The innovation processes can be flexible and adaptable, and form different configurations, depending on, e.g. the types of innovations and the circumstances of the organization. They can (a) form a fast track of selected processes; (b) have a non-linear sequence; (c) be iterative; (d) be implemented within, or independently from, other processes in the organization; and (e) be connected to other processes in the organization. The creative and experimentation processes focus on exploration to gain knowledge and can require resilience and flexibility. The innovation processes can interact and interrelate with other processes in the organization. e.g. research, product development, marketing, sales, partnering, mergers and acquisitions, collaboration, and intellectual property.*

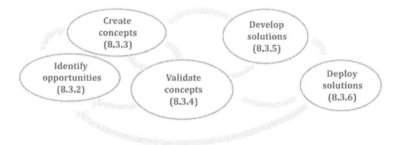

> *Identify Opportunities (Clause 8.3.2) can result in (a) An understanding of the potential value to be realized and other potential impacts; (b) Identified, defined, and prioritized opportunities, areas of opportunity or problem statements; and (c) An understanding of state of the art, including intellectual property rights.*
>
> *Create Concepts (Clause 8.3.3) can result in the (a) Concepts with preliminary value realization models that can be validated; (b) An understanding of the critical uncertainties or assumptions for each concept to be validated; and (c) an*

---

[11] ISO 56002:2019 – Innovation Management System - Guidance; July 2019.

initial assessment of risks, degree of novelty, and its implications for further development in terms of processes, structures, etc.

Validate Concepts (Clause 8.3.4) can result in (a) Validated concepts or proof of concepts with acceptable levels of uncertainty for further development; (b) relationships with users, customers, partners, and other interested parties; and (c) New knowledge.

Develop Solutions (Clause 8.3.5) results in (a) Developed solutions with value realization models, including value propositions; (b) Plans with established activities, resources, relationships, and timing for a full or phased deployment of the solutions; and (c) Fulfilment of deployment needs and requirements, including intellectual property rights considerations.

Deploy Solutions (Clause 8.3.6) results in (a) Realized value, financial or non-financial; (b) Impact in the form of adoption and new behaviors of users, customers, partners, and other interested parties; and (c) Insights and new knowledge to improve solutions.

Let's Summarize

The simplified *ideation to monetization* Innovation Value Chain, described in this chapter of the book can be used on a routine basis to address the growing needs of an organization. It is also applicable as a core execution engine in all the innovation types as discussed in Chapter-6. It can be adapted for crisis situation as discussed in Chapter-7. The steps will be iterative, more often than not. It takes a bit of practice to get good at executing the steps. In my experience, it takes about ten iterations, when you are doing it for the first time. After executing a few times, it would come down to 3-5 iterations. If you ever get it right the first time, then you are either God, or have already done something very similar, and it isn't innovation anymore.

Let's Take a Selfie

 # I believe we are good at

- ☐ Understanding the customer/market.
- ☐ Assessing the competition.
- ☐ Generating ideas.
- ☐ Screening and qualifying ideas.
- ☐ Making a business case.
- ☐ Executing a project.

 # Our typical ratio of funded projects to ideas generated is

- ☐ One Project for ~ More than 20 ideas.
- ☐ One Project for ~ 6-20 ideas.
- ☐ One Project for ~ 2-5 ideas.
- ☐ Someone tells us what to do.
- ☐ Don't know.

 # This is what we do with unfunded ideas or failed projects

- ☐ Trash/forget them.
- ☐ Capture them somewhere.
- ☐ Archive for future use in a database.
- ☐ Iterate a few times, archive in a searchable database, tagged with alerts.
- ☐ I am not sure.

 # About the ISO guidance on innovation management

- ☐ I am fully familiar with all 8 of them.
- ☐ I have heard about it, but not sure of access and applicability.
- ☐ I read it in this book for the first time and would like to know more.

2.   *Deep Market Insight*

DISCOVERY CONSISTS OF SEEING WHAT EVERYBODY HAS SEEN AND
THINKING WHAT NOBODY HAS THOUGHT.
– ALBERT SZENT-GYORGY

In 2016, I was brought in to accelerate new product development in a Business to Business (B2B) scenario. My client created advanced materials for the IT industry. They had some rare talent and know-how, but were struggling to compete on speed to market. Their material development cycle was typically 18-36 months, which was too long for their customer developing IT hardware, which goes obsolete in 24-36 months. They could never keep pace with the speed at which their B2B customer rolled out new products. A simple discovery session into their market insight process revealed the root cause. The Account Managers would wait for the Requests for Proposal (RFP) from the customer's purchasing department. By then, it was typically too late to address the development cycle time. My client needed the ability to forecast customer requirements at least a year ahead of the formal RFP in addition to accelerating the R&D activity.

Now, if you come to think of it, your customer just does not wake up one morning and issue an RFP. We all know, they work on it for a while! It is upon us to think like our customers or connect with them at their development roadmap level. So, an important new connection was put in place where the client's R&D head would connect with the R&D head of the B2B customer to capture customer insights at the forecast level; while, the marketing tracked the RFP. It gave my client the ability to deliver quality materials and gave them a competitive edge over almost 70% of their direct competitors, playing the speed to market game. On some very specific materials, they got exclusive development partnership programs to even offset part of the investment because of their unique engineering talent.

Since then I have successfully implemented this technique with a few other companies to build their innovation profile. It works very well.

> Market Insight is the primary differentiator
> between success and struggle of innovation.

There are multiple types of players in the marketplace. The most desirable type is the customer, who provides the primary pull to create new value. And the least desirable one is the competitor who creates cost and schedule pressure for survival in the market. At times, the competition is good, when it opens up a whole new market for you, which otherwise may be prohibitively expensive to enter. The third type of market player are the government regulators such as the Federal Aviation Administration, who exist for the public interest to control what comes to the market. Porter's five forces model also includes other two market players. First, product substitutes and new business entrants as threats to a business; and second the suppliers and partners who may have a bargaining power to influence your concept qualification.

A much deeper insight into all the marketplace forces is required to create a long-term roadmap, which we will cover in Volume-3. For now, let us understand how various innovation profiles look at customers and competitors during the initial phase of the Innovation Value Chain.

Customer Insight

As Theodore Levitt said, *"People do not want a quarter-inch drill, they want a quarter-inch hole."* Strategyn's *'Jobs to be Done'* Framework[12] centers around the concept that instead of thinking about what features or benefits a customer would want to buy, an innovation should instead try to

---

[12] Jobs to be Done: Theory to Practice; Anthony W. Ulwick; Book; 2016.

find out what job/activity/outcome a customer is trying to accomplish, and then develop something which helps them achieve that.

This way, you can develop an offering that a customer can 'hire' to complete their job. Office workers hire word-processing software to create documents. Surgeons hire scalpels to dissect soft tissue. But few companies keep this in mind while searching for ideas for breakthrough offerings. Simply asking people what jobs they have is unlikely to result in any insightful answers, as people themselves often don't realize or can't verbalize what they are trying to accomplish. What you need are insights, not opinions.

Any innovation project you undertake should start with an investigation of the potential jobs to be done for the customer. This step is most effective in the early stages of a project when the team goes out to look at how things currently run. This involves meeting real people, observing them in a neutral and unbiased way, and trying to get insights by learning about their behavior and frustrations, rather than their opinions.

What I am saying is that 'Voice of the Customer' is a term too simple to describe all that it entails. We should not assume that 'Voice of the Customer' is what the customer is asking for. We need to get into the customer's head, and understand what is in there, even if he or she cannot articulate it. That is customer insight, and it is captured differently for different innovation profiles.

According to ISO, **Insight** is defined as

> *'Profound and unique knowledge about an entity.' In the context of innovation activities, insights can reveal opportunities for the realization of value. Identifying insights is generally a part of the innovation processes. (ISO 56000:2020 Clause 3.4.3)*

To extend the definition, we can say that customer insight is a profound and unique knowledge about customer's pain points and desirable gains. Let us dig a little deeper into each of those, in the context of an innovation project.

Agile Followers

This is akin to traditional VOC. You search and understand the customer requirements, gather and analyze data, track and interpret RFPs, without substantial direct customer input. This is like listening to what the customer is asking for.

B2B Example: In the Aerospace industry, suppliers are led by the prime. As a supplier, your VOC efforts are to ferret out the prime's plans for the future with a concerted and coordinated effort to stay involved with the prime, and line up your ideas to address the well-defined needs.

Smart Forecasters

As a smart Forecaster, you ought to anticipate the customer requirements. This may involve gathering customer perspective or requirements by direct structured interviews, in anticipation of the formal RFP or other demand cycles. This is like watching the body language of the customer and understanding faint signals of desire or unarticulated needs.

In consumer products, the manufacturers drive the design fully and the role of VOC is to not just anticipate what the customer wants, but also to use that freedom to capture market share.

Case Study: Seagate[13] obtained higher-level market insights by analyzing patterns of customer 'voices' to surface unarticulated needs and then capitalized on that insight by formally presenting findings to key project owners and senior decision-makers. Seagate credited its successful launch of the U-Series X drive to its application of customer insight. By going directly to the end consumer (users of gaming consoles), Seagate was able to translate end-consumer voice and customer requirements into critical engineering specifications. The distinguishing elements were ...

---

[13] Generating Market Insight for Technology Prioritization; RTEC report Dec 2003;
Although the example is a bit dated, (~ 20 years old), the process is still relevant.

1. Cross-functional teams with primary responsibility in the hands of techies.
2. Rigorous interviewing skills training to drive the conversation away from 'problem-with-product' to understanding customers' overarching challenges.
3. VOC Program Manager role to steward the customer interaction process to identify new, 'whole solution' opportunities for Seagate.

Seagate designed VOC interview questionnaires to challenge customers to paint their ideal vision of the future to identify breakthrough opportunities. This is similar to the *'I wish'* ideation technique, discussed later in the book.

Visionary Trendsetters

As a Visionary Trendsetter, you lead the customer with what you believe is a value-add. It may involve observing the customer closely to understand usage and interactions better, and experimenting with a prototype, or beta release to a focus group of customer demographic. Analyzing customer products and services or end-users to understand pains and gains and developing a shared vision for the next generation products and working together on prototypes. This is like putting the words in the customer's mouth.

Of course, there are always small signals amidst a lot of noise. People like Bill Gates, Steve Jobs, Jeff Bezos, Mark Zuckerburg, and Elon Musk could hear very faint VOC, test their hypotheses, push the boundaries of innovation, and put words in the mouth of the customer.

So often, doing the common things uncommonly well or addressing what customers do not explicitly want can be disruptive.

Agile Followers **listen** to the customer.
Smart Forecasters **watch** the body language of the customer.
Visionary Trendsetters **whisper** into the ears of the customer.

Cry of the Customer

Graham Brown suggests that we should also consider the fact that often customers know what they do not want, even though they may fail to articulate what they want. Here are 3 examples:

1. Customers did not know they wanted Google, ... they just knew they did not want noisy directories like Yahoo!
2. Customers did not know they wanted TransferWise, ... they knew they did not want slow and expensive remittances!
3. Customers did not know they wanted Netflix, ... they knew they did not want late fees and limited movies!

Today, the digital transformation is making it easy to build small cross-functional teams that identify and respond fast to customer frustrations.

Steps to Capture Customer Insight

Hopefully, by now, it is apparent that customer insight is more than just VOC. You must aspire to understand what makes customers successful, not just satisfied. On many occasions, customers can not articulate their needs or are clueless about your capability to deliver. They show requirements that are a level lower than what they need. Best practices include building a team of marketing and domain experts, reaching out to the customer's customer, and gathering customer roadmap if practical. Government departments routinely share their vision. Many companies are willing to share their plans under a special type of non-disclosure of business arrangement. The steps below show various levels, providing progressively better insight.

1. Conduct data research and analysis, using tools such as Google, Government databases, 3rd party research databases.
2. Conduct discovery Interviews with standard questions, with a focus on listening rather than selling, getting to facts and not opinions, asking why?
3. Shadow and observe customer actions, reactions, emotions, feelings.
4. Immerse yourself in customer's daily life, and make a note of your actions, reactions, emotions, feelings.

5. Create a prototype or simulation and test your hypothesis or run the 'What if' conversation with customers.

More on Customer Insight

Customer insight is more than what product features or service performance the customers will receive during the transaction. It also involves delivery (how and where they receive it), consumption, and payment (how and when) aspects. Today, data is becoming a valuable commodity, and most of us do not keep it with us either. Online retailers are monetizing millennial's desire to not go to the shop, whatever the product.

Customer insight is more than a process in the marketing department to get customer input. It is intertwined with ongoing company engagement cultural improvements, and the most vital part of any innovation culture.

In summary, customer insight means much more than what the customer is asking for. It means interpreting what they would be willing to pay for. It helps understand the consumer, so your innovation has a better chance of market acceptance.

As an example, look at the difference between the success of Sony's Action Cam and GoPro action cameras. While Sony may deliver better quality videos, GoPro has been far more successful because it was designed to address customers' desire to film themselves in action. By giving users ways to mount the camera on helmets, bikes, even on their dogs, and to rapidly edit and share footage, GoPro solved a real problem. It fulfilled a conspicuous customer desire and subsequently won massive customer market share (48 percent to Sony's 8 percent in 2015, according to investment research and analytics company Market Realist. Robertson notes, *"Sony had every advantage in the marketplace, But GoPro started with what the customer wanted, and that's how they came out ahead."*

In 1975, living in the Himalayas, I had to walk up the hill to go to my middle school. It was tiring. There were no school buses in that small village. During one of the site visits to my father's construction site, I saw a conveyor belt carrying stones up the hill, with three or four long sections, to permit turning. I asked him, if we can put one of these by the roadside, so my friends and I can go uphill to the school. He encouraged me to think further and make a sketch. I got excited and took it on as a part of a science project. I got a disappointing 'F', claiming it to impractical, scary, and dangerous. My father helped me re-sketch and resubmit for a 'C'. I was happy even though the teacher did not seem to want me in her class. Today we call it an escalator and moving walkways or travelator. Imagine my delight when I saw it for the first time in 1992 entering the USA at the Atlanta airport.

Probably, the same reason no one wanted to sponsor my aerial food delivery toy in 1995. Something Amazon and UPS are pushing today.

The pandemic has suddenly pushed "contactless" as a key product differentiator for what the consumers will accept, whether it is a curbside pickup or a router installation in your home. While trying to rent out my condo, the advertisement stating 'schedule a touchless showing' attracted many takers.

Duality of Customer Insight

You would normally have multiple customers or stakeholders in an organization. They will have slightly different requirements. Sometimes their requirements are in conflict.

As a part of a new inspection systems design, we went in to observe and interview stakeholders. We started with the inspectors who will be using the equipment. They wanted to eliminate all pain associated with the inspection system's use. They wanted it to be easy to set up and learn, ergonomic and all-weather, clean with no consumables, having rapid and reliable response, and finally; easy to interpret and report to the boss. These appear obvious. On the other side, during the discussions with the business owners, we discovered they view it as a cost and would like to eliminate it. However, they had to live with it, for compliance and perhaps safety. So, we identified the primary needs of the systems must include both safety and economic value. Hence, we came up with a strategy for Industry 4.0 applications with Society 5.0 intent to define '*Safety 5.0*'.

Such situations require delicate handling and an approach that allows you to synthesize diverse requirements for acceptance of the innovation in the marketplace.

Competitive Insight

Once again, the frequently used term **competitive benchmarking** is too simple to describe all that it entails. We should not assume that it refers only to what the competitor is selling in the market today. We need to understand that in the context of customer insight in order to gain and sustain the competitive advantage. That is competitive insight, and it is captured differently for different innovation profiles.

Let us dig a little deeper into each of those, in the context of competitive insight for any project on hand.

Agile Followers

Essentially, there are two fundamental parameters to compete on: price, and product/service features or Key Performance Indicators (KPIs). *Agile Followers* must routinely perform *Competitive Benchmarking, i.e.* comparing your current offerings with those of your competitors. The KPIs that are important to the customer can be tabulated, plotted, sorted, and compared to help define your target offering. Unfortunately, they are in a visible race on a well-known turf, once the customer requirements are clear and open to everyone in the marketplace.

Smart Forecasters

Smart Forecasters must be able to predict their competitors next offering based on Political, Economic, Social, Technical, Environmental, and Legal trends (PESTEL) and build their offering accordingly. Today, you might want to add Pandemic to the PESTEL trends as well. These companies must benchmark talent, know-how, technology, and any relevant internal parameters today that will differentiate them externally tomorrow. They need competitive intelligence.

Visionary Trendsetters

Trendsetters just make the competition irrelevant. Being the trendsetter, if you are far ahead on customer insight, then you can be the market leader. There may be no competition. It, of course, raises a question of whether you are thinking on correct lines, or are ahead of your time, which could be high risk. You may get rejected.

Significant competitive intelligence required to build a product roadmap will be discussed in Volume-3. However, in the context of a single project or an initiative, direct analysis of limited data might be enough, for now.

Agile Followers rely on **competitive benchmarking** of product parameters. *Smart Forecaster* go for **competitive intelligence** of what's coming next. *Visionary Trendsetters* make **competition irrelevant.**

Regulatory Forces

Before you can take your new product or service to the market, you must address all applicable regulatory concerns. There are many US federal regulatory agencies to ensure human safety, security, and in many cases integrity of corporations. The top few include ...

CDC   Center for Disease Control

CPSC   Consumer Product Safety Commission enforces federal safety standards for consumer goods.

EPA   Environmental Protection Agency establishes and enforces pollution standards.

EEOC   Equal Employment Opportunity Commission administers and enforces Title VIII of the Civil Rights Act of 1964 (fair employment).

FAA   Federal Aviation Administration regulates and promotes air transportation safety, including airports and pilot licensing.

FCC   Federal Communications Commission regulates interstate and foreign communication by radio, telephone, telegraph, and television.

FDIC   Federal Deposit Insurance Corporation insures bank deposits, approves mergers, and audits banking practices.

FED   Federal Reserve System regulates banking; manages the money supply.

FERC   Federal Energy Regulatory Commission Fixes rates and regulates the interstate transportation and sale of electricity, oil, and natural gas.

FTC   Federal Trade Commission ensures free and fair competition and protects consumers from unfair or deceptive practices.

FDA   Food and Drug Administration administers federal food purity laws, drug testing and safety, and cosmetics.

ICC   Interstate Commerce Commission enforces federal laws concerning transportation that crosses state lines.

NHTSA National Highway Traffic Safety Administration sets and enforces laws to promote motor vehicle safety and to protect drivers, passengers, and pedestrians.

NLRB   National Labor Relations Board prevents or corrects unfair labor practices by either employers or unions.

NRC   Nuclear Regulatory Commission licenses and regulates non-military nuclear facilities.

OSHA Occupational Safety and Health Administration develops and enforces federal standards and regulations ensuring working conditions.

SEC   Securities and Exchange Commission administers federal laws concerning the buying and selling of securities.

Innovation and regulations are at odds with each other to provide the required check and balance for safe and acceptable evolution of systems for public use. While innovations are leading and exploratory in nature, regulations are lagging and controlling by design. Regulations lag because they are based on data and experience. They are written to avoid harmful application of innovative ideas. Innovations are generally an exception to status quo, whereas regulations leave no room for exception. If marketplace is like a car, then innovative companies are the engine to drive it forward (social evolution) and regulations are like a brake[14] to avoid an accident (an unsafe product entering the market).

An interesting unconfirmed story of innovation and regulation comes from the recent manned SpaceX launch. The Dragon crew went to the International Space Station and returned back to earth using primarily an automated system; but they were denied the use of Tesla self-driving car to go from ready room to the launch pad.

Let's Summarize

The single most important differentiating factor in the success of an innovation initiative is the user/customer insight and the options to address their needs and wants. As you can see that your profile is closely tied, rather defined, by the approach you take towards market insight.

---

[14] The analogy of brakes and car in a blog at https://crypticvaibhav.wordpress.com/2010/08/02/brakes/

Let's Take a Selfie

 # I am focus on the drill machine (the product) as compared to the hole (the job)

- ☐ Never to sometimes.
- ☐ Depends upon the situation.
- ☐ Often to always.

 # Our top 5 customers are listed here and I have 'x' marked those where I know their growth plans.

- ☐ __
- ☐ __
- ☐ __
- ☐ __
- ☐ __

 # Our top 3 competitors are listed here and I have 'x' marked those where I know their growth plans.

- ☐ __
- ☐ __
- ☐ __

 # I can at least think of one instance, where we are educating the regulatory body to drive a trendsetting innovation.

- ☐ __

 # I can at least think of one instance, where we are collaborating with our competitor.

- ☐ __

3.   *Structured Ideation*

For decades, my peers vouched for me to be an idea guy. In 2016, I met Bryan Mattimore[15] who is a master ideation facilitator. We worked on a project through CalTech for a global chemical company. I spent many days with him learning and watching him in action and reached a whole new level of appreciation around creating ideas. Bryan is a "master facilitator" who can make a group of ordinary people generate extraordinary ideas within a few hours. He uses idea triggers and empowers the group to build upon each other's output. Over the last 2 years, we have explored some novel ways of combining ideation techniques with building business models, which have now been weaved in this chapter.

According to British Standards[16]: An **Idea** is defined as *"a result of mental activity that is a process, product, device, or artistic work."*

According to d.school Stanford[17] *"Ideation is the mode of the design process in which you concentrate on idea generation. Mentally, it represents a process of 'going wide' in terms of concepts and outcomes. Ideation provides both the fuel and also the source material for building prototypes and getting innovative solutions into the hands of your users. You ideate in*

---

[15] Author of the book "Idea Stormers."

[16] Specification for the Provision of Services Relating to the Commercialization of Intellectual Property Rights; BS 8538:2011.

[17] An Introduction to Design Thinking, ModeGuideBOOTCAMP2010.pdf; The Hasso Plattner Institute of Design at Stanford, commonly known as the d.school.

order to transition from identifying problems to creating solutions for your users. Ideation is your chance to combine the understanding you have of the problem space and people you are designing for with your imagination to generate solution concepts. Particularly early in a design project, ideation is about pushing for a widest possible range of ideas from which you can select, not simply finding a single, best solution."

> *According to ISO, Ideation is a 'process of generating, sharing, and evolving ideas and concepts.' An idea is a basic element of thought that can be either concrete, or abstract. Ideation is generally part of the innovation processes (ISO56000:2020 Clause 3.6.3)*

Ideation, Not Just Brainstorming

Traditional brainstorming method involves a group of individuals thinking freely. Some of its characteristics limit its effectiveness. You get insufficient participation from introverts, and generally a few participants dominate the conversation. The concept of withholding judgment, hinders others from building on the original idea. Many times, group-think takes over, and blocks the fresh juices from coming in. And then without an external trigger, the entire exercise ends up generating a few average ideas around a couple of dominating themes. Also, traditionally, people start voting on ideas at the end of a session and that promotes mediocrity. Best of the ideas are understood by few people and they get voted down, whereas maximum votes go to those that are obvious and incremental in nature.

Ideation can be viewed as brainstorming on steroids, or an evolved version of the traditional brainstorm. It begins with a clearly defined challenge problem for the session, brings structure and technique, uses triggers to stimulate ideas, and eliminates the influence of a minority of participants. It brings in quality and quantity, allows others to build on inputs in the spirit of collaboration, and directly addresses the group-think psychology. Ideation is a technique that involves both the left and right sides of the brain to allow breakthroughs from entrenched habits of thought and persistent difficult problems.

Both brainstorming and ideation require a detached and trained facilitator working with the group, and a mechanism to capture and filter ideas. Affinity techniques or idea clustering to generate themes is generally more valuable than voting on individual ideas. The themes can then be used to create a few value propositions.

Structured Ideation helps ask the right questions, brings together perspectives and strengths of the participating members, takes steps beyond the obvious solutions and therefore increases the innovation potential of your solution, through volume and variety.

Planning an Ideation Session

Objective(s)

While you need out-of-the-box thinking during the ideation session, you need a fairly well-defined box when it comes to defining the challenge problem or the objective of the session. These objectives can be at any level – purpose, strategic, tactical, operational, project subject matter, etc. The objectives are typically focused on how and/or what; and occasionally on discovering the purpose (why). Some examples include …

- How can we save corals and marine life from chemical waste (purpose)?
- How do we use Industry 4.0 for the development of a special child (purpose)?
- How to go through digital transformation in the next 3 years (strategic)?
- What will be the impact of industry 4.0 on our business (strategic)?
- How to grow the business by 5X in 5Years (strategic)?
- How to expand the market in the Asia Pacific region (tactical)?
- How can we design a compact high temp storage box (technical)?
- How to reduce the component weight by 22% (technical)?
- How to recover from schedule variance (operational)?
- What can we do to help the customer accelerate production (tactical)?
- What set of technologies can we develop for a smart home market (technical/strategic)?

If the objective is too large or broad, then I suggest a series of sessions, structured hierarchically. A theme (from a cluster of ideas) at the strategic level becomes an objective at the tactical level. For example, the executive team gets together for an ideation session with the objective 'How to grow the business by 5X over the next 5 years?' The outcome is a set of 6 idea themes, and 4 of them become follow-up ideation objectives.

- *Objective*: How to grow the business by 5X in 5Years (strategic)?

  o *Sub-objective 1*: Adapt Industry 4.0?
    - Launch an Artificial Intelligence enabled service.
    - Offer augmented reality-based training.
  o *Sub-objective 2*: Expand the business into the Asia Pacific region.
    - Set up a partnership with a university in Singapore.
    - Acquire and turnaround a struggling small business in India.
  o *Sub-objective 3*: Scout & acquire training company on ISO9001.
  o *Sub-objective 4:* How will Amazon/Google impact our business.
  o *Sub-objective 5/ 6*: Not worth pursuing.

Every objective statement should have a unique topic-owner. The facilitator and the topic owner should be empowered to modify the problem statement within a narrow boundary.

Given that we are in the middle of the 4th industrial revolution, every company today should run ideation sessions with these types of objectives.

- What are the opportunities or threats from industry 4.0 technologies?
- What company values will drive our socio-economic development?
- What ideas or industry 4.0 technologies can help us create value for the society; or perhaps help in progress towards UN's SDGs?
- What new skills do we need to thrive through this transformation?
- What new business models may bring us additional value or stability?

Companies such as Amazon, Apple, Facebook, and Google, are on a roll to change the world. Their moves can suddenly disrupt your business, and ideation around those is important, just like you plan your house for storms, well in advance.

As we emerge out of the Coronavirus pandemic, some plausible ideation objectives could be ...

- How will consumer behavior change in the next 3 to 5 years?
- What is the impact of unemployment surge to long-term demand for your products and services?
- Which markets will disappear for you and which ones will expand rapidly?

Ideation objectives have a strong linkage with the innovation profile.

> *Agile Followers* define ideation objectives based on VOC or RFP.
> *Smart Forecasters* defined their objectives based on anticipated needs.
> *Visionary Trendsetters* pick up a social or professional white space and often take a moon shot.

Identification of funding sources can be a part of the ideation exercise. Care should be taken not to use that as an excuse to pre-screen some good ideas. I normally prefer to keep funding conversation as a follow-on topic.

Participants

The most important member in an ideation session is the facilitator. A good facilitator has some knowledge of the subject matter without bias in favor of any outcome, is a good communicator, is assertive in managing the group dynamics, is respectful of group diversity, can scribe inputs and engage with individuals at the same time, and has a sense of humor. Most importantly a competent facilitator understands multiple ideation techniques and tricks to continuously trigger fresh ideas.

Innovation coaches often make good ideation facilitators, unlike innovation management consultants. A consultant solves the problem, whereas a coach helps build your competency to solve the problem. An ideation session facilitated by a coach provides the team with techniques to generate and refine ideas, which are useful after the session is over.

Sometimes, you may feel that you can generate ideas faster when you work alone. However, if you want creativity, resist that temptation. Do it as a group, preferably a diverse group. Diversity of skills and roles is a key design element. There is no 'right size' for the group, but in my experience 5-15 people is the sweet spot. There is no perfect composition of the group. I typically start with a core group of product/service developers and business development personnel who will have to later execute. I always suggest bringing in an IT person (it is the digital age after all) and a student/intern (who can have wild thoughts). Sometimes, I add a finance person to put some reality into the solutions.

It is also important to keep a few elements out of the session. I try to keep idea-killers, naysayers, and heavyweight executives out of the session, whose presence may intimidate participants. If a particular senior staff member insists on participating, then it is an indicator to exclude them (!). A smart facilitator may compensate for such undesirable engagement, but I do not count on it.

Ideation Techniques

There are several ideation techniques, and research on the topic is producing new methods and tricks all the time. Bryan Mattimore has compiled over 20 of these in his book[18], which I would say is a must-read for all ideation facilitators. Some of these techniques are discussed in brief later on in this chapter.

Based on the objective and participants, the facilitator should select a primary and couple of supplementary ideation techniques for the session, and plan on training the participants on the techniques. The choice of technique depends upon group size, facilitator understanding of the technique and the objective as well. It will become clear when we discuss those techniques.

---

[18] Idea Stormers – How to Lead and Inspire Creative Breakthroughs; Bryan W. Mattimore; Book, 2012.

Place and Duration

It is best to conduct an ideation session in a new setting, preferably a stimulating ambiance, with articles that can provide visual triggers, such as unconventional furniture, lighting, toys. Keep an ample amount of wall space to display growing content. And of course, an unlimited supply of water, coffee, and fresh fruits or preferred refreshments. It is important to be relaxed and not distracted by smartphones. I have seen some really superb ideas hit the happy hour table, once the formal sessions are closed out. There is no reason to exclude that additional input.

Again, there is no single answer to how long should this be scheduled. I typically plan for 2-4 hours for a fairly well-defined objective, depending upon the group size. Sometimes, a full-day is warranted, anything beyond that is likely to produce diminishing results and calls for a hierarchical session set.

Executing an Ideation Session

Kick-off

The facilitator should kick-off the session with the agenda below as minimum:

1. **Self-introduction** of all team members with a personal non-work story.
2. **Quick training** of the ideation technique(s) and rules of engagement.
3. Broader **context** and clear **problem statement (objective).**

Process

The facilitator should use the ideation technique and tool, to generate and capture a large number of ideas. These ideas are then clustered under some obvious themes as they emerge, permitting a many to many mapping (one idea multiple themes, a theme has multiple ideas). As a team, pick a few promising themes, and begin creating value propositions right away. If not, take that as a homework and bring the filled value proposition sheets during a follow-up session. The follow up session could take the shape of an ideation session, a review meeting, or a Dolphin Tank (discussed later).

Various Roles

Kotler and Trias de Bes have defined 6 different roles during ideation[19]. These do not need to play part in a specific sequence and all of them may also not be required all the time.

(A) Activators initiate the innovation process, without worrying about stages or phases.

(B) Browsers supply the group with information relevant both to the start of the process and to the application of new ideas.

(C) Creators ideate new concepts and possibilities and search for new solutions at any point in the process.

(D) Developers turn ideas into products, services, solutions, or marketing plans.

(E) Executors take care of everything to do with implementation and execution.

(F) Facilitators approve the new spending items and investment needed as the innovation process moves forward. They also manage the process to prevent it from getting stuck. The term facilitator used here is more of a sponsor and should not be confused with the facilitator of the ideation exercise.

Ideation Techniques

In this section, we cover five of the most effective ideation techniques from the 'Idea Stormers' book, that I have enjoyed over the years. Readers may refer to the source[20] for full details as well as many other possible techniques.

---

[19] "A-to-F Method for Innovation Success", Philip Kotler and Fernando Trias de Bes; Book; 2011.
[20] "Idea Stormers – How to lead and inspire creative breakthroughs" Bryan Mattimore, Book 2012.

I Wish ...

Technique: 'I Wish' begins with the assumption that anything is possible. Money, energy, time are all available in abundance, as if you can have whatever you can imagine, and even break the laws of nature. This helps move beyond the limiting constraints of reality. The paradox of the 'I wish technique' is that it is only by first considering the impossible that we can know the outer limits of what is possible, and therefore identify potentially the most exciting ideas. Typically, the output from the 'wishing' session will be entirely new and original points of view, and concepts.

Facilitation: Go around the room with everyone expressing one item at a time in the form of a statement 'I wish ....' Facilitator can encourage the participants to think and say the impossible by thinking and saying the impossible himself or herself. Keep going around until everyone is feeling exhausted with their list. Allow the participants to build on existing items. Now go back to several of the most interesting and/or far out wishes and try to turn the impossible into the portions that are possible. Keep working through the list of wishes until you have generated a few new exciting and practical ideas.

Example: In response to the recent pandemic, while under 'Stay at Home' orders, my family played this twice. Here is the list of five favorites

1. I wish we could rinse the mouth with a concoction while handwashing.
2. I wish we could do an ultraviolet sweep treatment of entire streets.
3. I wish we could wear a dental brace that will attract viruses at the mouth.
4. I wish we could kill the virus with certain musical frequencies like the chanting of 'OM.'
5. I wish we could mutate the virus with a spice into a less harmful virus.

Extension: This technique can be curated to create company strategy as well through the following 3 steps.

1. Split the collated 'wishes' into three horizons: near, mid, and far-term.
2. Validate with market data and trends.
3. Build-in stress checkpoints.

Visual Triggers

Technique: Recall my personal story of how a conveyor belt triggered the idea of a travellator type device. That is a classic case of a visual trigger. Visual stimuli are a great way of coming up with ideas for your challenge problem. The mind grasps on images and videos much faster than words from other people around the table, as about half of the brain's cognitive capacity is evolved for the sense of vision. Google, YouTube, wiki, etc. are vast repositories of visuals which can be used to trigger ideas. I use Google Images all the time to search for ideas.

Facilitation: Start with 2-3 keywords in the opportunity/problem statement and define 6-10 synonyms and antonyms. Search through Google Images using the keywords and scroll through the 100s of options, slowly. Let participants note down the ideas as they scan through. Then go back and solicit what the participants noted. Discuss, or redirect searches as required.

Example: Once ideating around the conceptual design of an autonomous bridge inspection device, we used Google Images as triggers. We found 17 possible land, water, and airborne configurations already. Then we tried bridge construction and repair, to discover many more. After browsing some links through the initial pictures, we listed almost 35 possible configurations. The most interesting ones were hybrid ones; 8-legged spider with wheels on 4 of them, or a 4-wheel small truck with a platform for drone landing.

Problem Inversion

Technique: Here you read the objective as if it were a solution and define what could have been the problem. Now start ideating around this higher-level problem.

Facilitation: Write down the problem statement as a solution. Define two to three possible higher-level problems. Divide the group into three subgroups. Let each group now generate multiple possible solutions to each of the problem statement. Discuss and screen options.

A belief behind this is, 'Every problem is a solution to something, and every solution is a problem for something.'

Example: Penguins at a local aquarium were suffering from bumble foot. The attempted solution using 3D printed sandals was not working. I was invited to facilitate an ideation session with problem defined as 'How to redesign the sandals so the penguins stay on their feet while the bird heals.' If you step back and look at the situation, the 3D printed sandals are a solution to the problem 'How do we allow ointments to heal the penguin feet.' During ideation the group identified the root cause as lack of feet hardening while growing up in a soft incubator during early months. One of the ideas appeared to be a redesign of the incubator rather than the sandal, to alleviate the root cause.

Problem Redefinition

Technique: Problem redefinition is a great way for business model innovation. It helps you invent new ways of looking at your value proposition. Words bring their creative limitations with them. The kind and quality of ideas generated to solve a problem is often influenced by the way it is defined.

Facilitation: Write down your current value proposition. *e.g.*

We ...*create*... and ...*sell it*... through ...*channel*... to ...*them*...

Split the statement into multiple action pieces and participating entities, as shown above in *italics.* Generate multiple alternatives for each of those and put them back in the statement to create several alternate problem statement or value propositions.

We ...*assemble*... and ...*lease it*... through ...*retail store*... to ...*them*...

If you have 4 elements with 10 alternate options, you just created 10,000 combinations and most of them will not make much sense to you, yet. You need to screen and select the few that make sense for further evaluation. You can keep coming back to the discards for opportunities that time, circumstances, and new technology open up. Or someone else can make it work.

Example: During an ideation session, we wrote down the current business for a specific sensor as in the gray line. Down below we listed options for each

Attribute	Channel	Deliver	To	Application
Currently	Sales dept	Sell	Govt	Weight
Alternatives	Distributor	Finance	Industrial	Location
	e-commerce	Service	Space	Corrosion
	Partners	Subscription	Transportation	Noise
		Lease/Rent	Health care	
		Time-Share	Cell phone	Impurity
		Buy back	Vets	Vibration
		Upgrade	Automotive	
			Household	

There are now 3x7x8x5 = 840 combinations, and at least 50 of them are feasible. The team eventually explored 6 of them and put 2 in practice to boost their market share.

Questioning Assumptions

Technique: As a way to maintain sanity in the world, we naturally make assumptions about how the world operates. However, from an idea-generating standpoint, it's often useful to question the most basic assumptions about product/service, your organization, marketplace, political, and social trends, etc.

Facilitation: Go around the room and generate a list of 20-30 items, that participants feel they typically assume around the topic. Once everyone has exhausted their thought, push them to go deeper in the back of their minds to get to those hard assumptions that so deep that they are not even consciously aware of them. These are generally the most valuable items. Take a brief break to freshen up the mind for the next step. Now, go back through each assumption and try to generate novel ideas/alternative ways of looking at the problem based on the newly-questioned assumption. The break is important since the two steps require different mental activities.

This technique is powerful when handled with care. Not all assumptions made by the team are true, but they may still be worth addressing.

Example: Here are some very common assumptions that I come across in almost all ideation sessions:

- Management will never approve this until ____
- If this does not work, we will have to ____
- Customer will never accept this ____
- There is no budget to buy ____
- We are not allowed to ____
- Our business model is ____
- This is too dangerous ____

Open Ideation

The *Forecasters* and *Trendsetters* do extensive open ideation, sourced both internally and externally, gaining competitive advantage.

Internal Sourcing – Dolphin Tank

Technique: This ideation tool is a derivative of "Shark Tank" type meetings, except that instead of sharks, we have friendly Dolphins. These experts will nurture and mentor ideas from anyone in the organization, in the spirit of Open Innovation and broad engagement.

Facilitation: Define and announce the problem/objective or keep it open within the strategic objectives or purpose. Identify 3-5 Dolphins, competent to evaluate ideas for the problem identified. Identify a date and open the submission to all employees, as a broad announcement. Let them come with an idea and present it in a 3-5-minute pitch. Discuss and evaluate the idea for further actions. Provide feedback on what still can be done to refine. The objective is not to eat up like a shark, but provide tender love and care to help build the culture of promoting open ideation.

This is also a good tool to apply at regular intervals for building the innovation culture and mindset (Volume-4).

Example: I have successfully used this on several occasions across multiple companies. It is typically met with an apprehension among participants, but this gets better after 2 to 3 rounds. With one of the power sector small business, I have heard that they were able to launch two new product derivatives. I have a feeling that there must have been a bit of a shark somewhere, else they could have seen a new product.

External Sourcing

Ideas can be harvested from network partners (sister business units, suppliers, universities), market (customer insight, competitive intel), formal technology scouting (startups, patent monitoring, conferences) business arrangement (acquisition, joint ventures, licensing) and freelance consultants who work across domains.

University COE: Many corporations run Centers of Excellence at universities with sustained funding, focused on a mixed bag of objectives – some clearly defined and some open-ended. E.g. Daimler Chrysler, Hewlett Packard, Boeing, General Motors, United Technologies (Now Raytheon), all have university centers.

Consortium: On many occasions' companies come together to fund some basic development work and follow-up with an inhouse application. E.g. MIT's computing alliance, Auto industry's Global Human Body Models Consortium, and the Integrative Materials Design Center at Worcester Polytechnic Institute.

Web collection portals: Many companies have successfully tried to "crowdsource" ideas from the public through websites, e.g. Innocentive.

Supplier partnering: A fairly successful model and my personal favorite is to engage your suppliers in helping you ideate and innovate. E.g.

Nike, P&G, Whirlpool, have all successfully partnered and rewarded their suppliers.

Customers: While we are looking at suppliers, we could also tap our customers. A joint session on their requirements helps generate ideas that are pre-sold.

Ideation Kitchen

You may choose to create a dedicated space for ideation with unconventional facility. Some of the important ingredients to generate tons of ideas are listed here …

- **Ambiance** – Space with unconventional, artistic, multi-functional, nature blended, and artifacts to set the mood, and open the mind to possibilities.
- **Catalysts** – Facilitator, Subject Matter Experts, stimulators, stirrers to trigger new thoughts and help sort out confusion.
- **Process** – for ideation, filtration, validation, and Intellectual Property (IP) for efficient and effective use of resources.
- **Toys & tools** – Games, audio-visual, 3D printer, analysis, testbeds, and prototyping capabilities to quickly test the hypothesis.
- **Clear discomfort** with the current state through challenging messaging pushing you hard to come with novel approach.

Each of these is important. In my experience, missing any of them significantly reduces the quality and quantity of ideas generated.

Beyond Idea Generation

Ideation management is more than generating a large quantity of ideas.

Novelty and Heresy

Paul Graham[21] has recently shared his perspective on mining novel ideas around a heresy. To discover new things, you have to come up with good ideas that are non-obvious. A common way for a good idea to be non-obvious is for it to be concealed by a popular assumption. And this brings a lot of opposition from people attached to the mistaken assumption, Galileo and Darwin being two examples. So, an organization or society hurts itself with a culture of pouncing on a heresy, by trying to protect that assumption. You also suppress any idea that implies indirectly that it is false. Over a period of time, every cherished mistaken assumption builds a dead zone of unexplored ideas around it. And the more preposterous the assumption, the bigger the dead zone it creates. Which also means that one way to find new ideas is to look around the heresies.

Ideas from Artificial Intelligence

Ryan Abbott's group out of the University of Surrey has created an artificial intelligence named DABUS[22]. Using a first system of neural networks to generate new ideas, and second system of networks to determine novelty and consequences. The net can selectively form and ripe ideas having most novelty, utility, and value. DABUS invented a beverage container and a flashing device used for search and rescue that became a subject of patent applications in the United States and Europe. It has been declined opening a debate around who/what may be an inventor on a patent?

Abbott asserts the need for and benefit of AI in solving many of the world's problems, such as curing diseases and reversing climate change.

---

[21] Novelty and Hersey; http://www.paulgraham.com/nov.html; Blogpost Nov 2019.
[22] What is DABUS? http://imagination-engines.com/iei_dabus.php.

Abbott[23] sees the current patent laws as an obstruction to such potential developments, stating, "If outdated IP laws around the world don't respond quickly to the rise of the inventive machine, the lack of incentive for AI developers could stand in the way of a new era of spectacular human endeavor."

Virtual Ideation

When Coronavirus Pandemic forced millions to work from home in early 2020, we went virtual with ideation techniques, something that even I had not supported until this time. My very first experiment using Zoom™ worked satisfactorily. Within a couple of ideation sessions, we understood how to facilitate virtual ideation. Ann Gynn of Content Marketing Institute provided a very simple and useful guidance on processes, tips, and tools for brainstorming in the remote world[24]. Beyond Google, there are applications and tools like Ideaboardz, Lucidchart, Miro, Mural, Otter.ai, Slack, Trello, and Ziteboard which can aid virtual ideation.

Virtual ideation is a useful process to master as we continue with global collaboration, slowly becoming a norm to handle tough problems. My assumptions around the topic have been challenged and I am glad I am past that mental block and open to virtual ideation. I can now safely conceive a virtual reality based collaborative ideation tool in the market.

Screening Ideas

One of my clients was struggling to change the culture from highly risk-averse to somewhat innovative. The executive in charge allocated a special area for innovation – a large conference room. For a long time, it was referred to as *war room*; indicating high-stress zone, near-term fix-it

---

[23] Artificial Intelligence Inventor Asks If 'WHO' can be an Inventor is the Wrong Question? Benjamin Ford; Aug 2019; https://www.ipwatchdog.com/2019/08/05/artificial-intelligence-inventor-asks-whether-can-inventor-wrong-question

[24] 25 Tools and Ideas for Brainstorming in a Remote World; Ann Gynn; April 9, 2020; https://contentmarketinginstitute.com/2020/04/brainstorm-content-ideas-remotely/

attitude; that I was very uncomfortable with. After a few urges, the team agreed to re-name the conference room. Twelve of us got together and started putting keywords on the wall. After 30 minutes we had about 30 words to choose from, each one reflecting a certain emotion or mindset. Then came the voting round, without the benefit of discussion or logic. In the end, the room was named '*Innovation Fort*' rather than 'Possibilities Lab' or 'Open Sky Room' or 'Blue Ocean View'. To me it was immediately apparent that most people are threatened by innovation and gravitated towards a 'safety zone'. A great example of how voting can lead to an average and most common belief, rather than, an aggressive, forward-looking, hard to work through, but high-value choice.

I have seen time and again that the best of the ideas does not get enough votes, simply because they are not well understood by most. The truly visionary thoughts will probably get only one vote, that of the originator.

A simple process of voting on ideas in a democratic style drives mediocrity. Promising futuristic ideas will probably not be understood by most and rejected during the voting process. Simplest and common denominators will typically get more votes.

Voting with a pre-defined criterion is a better way, as long as the team has time and intellect to discuss and caucus the impact. A much better approach is to cluster all generated ideas under a few selected themes and work through the value proposition as discussed in the next chapter at the theme level.

Have you watched how the company grows faster under the founder's entrepreneurial mindset? And when it is in the hands of a management team, it stalls and begins to behave like an average company! Ever wonder what happened? It got democratized and decisions are now based on a commonly accepted approach.

Idea Robbers[25]

Like many other innovators, you explain your idea to your friends, colleagues, or superiors trying to get funding or valuable feedback. But then, weeks or months later, you found out that someone realized your idea without your permission. There are so many similar stories and the point is that often you cannot do much except to feel miserable and helpless. Is it a good idea to take someone's idea?

A stolen or transferred idea is a closed box. The 'idea-recipient' does not know that there may be some other related ideas behind it. What could be the next features? Which combinations can be done with other sectors of the market? Also, the innovator was in some state-of-mind when the idea was born and she can recall this memory (or at least try to recall it) and sometimes continue in the same direction as during the time of idea generation. The 'idea-recipient' cannot have this possibility. Also, the innovator knows how this idea could grow and how the next project might be built upon this idea.

The thief or copycat or surrogate will never find out all of the ideas that might come afterwards. The stolen or borrowed or inherited idea often remains in the shape it had at the beginning without any new valuable additions. Finally, an 'idea-recipient' can never know all future features of the original idea that the innovator already has in his head (or in her notebook).

So, if your idea is stolen, borrowed, or handed over, you are still the best person to make a better project/product. On similar lines, I always encourage my client leadership to let the idea originator lead the development or at least be a key member of the development team.

---

[25] The Case of the Stolen Idea; Tomislav Buljubasi, Disruptor League (Innovation Excellence); https://disruptorleague.com/2018/06/07/the-case-of-the-stolen-idea/ ; June 2018.

Ernest Hughes[26] says, *"An idea is not responsible for the people that believe in it. So, the part about logistics is to move the idea around until it finds people that believe in it."* In some instances, I have seen that the idea originator may choose to pass it on to someone else. It usually works out best for all parties when cooperation is chosen over stealing.

Idea Killers

Employees are closer to the problem and the customer and are best placed to create ideas. They generate new and useful ideas all the time, quite often to meet their boss Mr. Anti-idea Manager. Killing ideas is a mindset issue.

Here is how it sounds like (and what it often means)

- Fill out the ideation form (I don't have time for you).
- Bring it up at the next quarterly all hands (Let someone else kill it).
- We have tried this and failed (I am smarter than you).
- Is my competition doing this? (I can't take a chance).
- Let me play devil's advocate (The devil in me is talking).

Some classic examples of employee ideas that took companies to new growth levels include 3M's post-it note, British Airways fuel cost savings by decreasing the number of toilet-pipes on flights, AdSense at Google, and Amazon Prime.

Promoting Ideas

Semmelweis Effect[27] - The tendency for people to reject new evidence that contradicts established beliefs.

The effect gets its name from the story of Ignaz Semmelweis, the Hungarian doctor who pioneered hand washing to prevent infections in

---

[26] https://edison365.com/wp-content/uploads/2019/10/IB-ep.06-Ernest-Hughes-transcript.pdf
[27] The Semmelweis Myth and Why It's Not Really True; https://www.digitaltonto.com/2018/the-semmelweis-myth-and-why-its-not-really-true/; July 8, 2018.

hospitals during the 1840s. However, he was unable to get the medical establishment to accept his idea. Thousands, if not millions, died unnecessarily because of the establishment dragging their feet and rejecting the idea. The Semmelweis effect is very real. We do get trapped in existing paradigms and that often blinds us to important new information.

The hospital that Semmelweis worked in, had quite a high maternal mortality rate, the typical symptoms being high fever after delivering the baby. Semmelweis' key insight came when his friend, Jakob Kolletschka, was pricked with a scalpel during an autopsy and soon came down with symptoms much like the women in the maternity ward. Semmelweis inferred that the medical students must be transferring 'cadaverous particles' to the maternity patients and instituted a strict regime of hand washing. Mortality rates fell dramatically. Yet instead of being lauded for his accomplishment, Semmelweis soon found himself castigated and considered a quack. Frustrated, Semmelweis wrote angry letters to prominent physicians. That, along with the political events at the time, led to his dismissal from the hospital. His mental state steadily declined, and he was eventually confined to a medical institution, where he died, in morbid irony, from an infection he contracted under care. Semmelweis, thinking his results were clear enough, did not see the value in communicating his work effectively, formatting his publications clearly, or even collecting data in a manner that would gain his ideas greater acceptance. Luckily, those that came later, like Louis Pasteur, Joseph Lister, and Robert Koch were more attentive and helped establish the germ theory of disease. The truth is that ideas alone, even breakthrough ideas, rarely amount to much. Innovations also need to be communicated effectively if they are to spread and make an impact on society.

Every innovator encounters resistance. The ones that succeed are not necessarily smarter or more talented than the others but learn to overcome obstacles they find in their paths. In the end, that's what makes the difference.

> If your idea is important enough,
> then it is your job to see it through.

Presenting Ideas

The basic and most popular way people express ideas are through a statement, or a sketch. Some will say, you should prepare an elevator pitch – 30 seconds of verbal text. I like two other options:

Bryan Mattimore's Billboard[28]: covering (1) The single most important benefit from customer eye as a headline in text, (2) A visual, and (3) A reason to believe or a call to action. Highway billboards, ignoring their being an environmental eyesore, are one of the most concise forms of communication. Creating a memorable and motivating piece of communication that has only a second or two to make an impact certainly requires both brevity and clarity of thought.

Alexander Osterwalder's, Value Proposition Canvas[29]: covering (1) jobs to be done, (2) Pains and pain relievers, and (3) gain creators and gains. Value Proposition Canvas is the best way to iterate and refine. Once you are satisfied with the solution, you can also use Billboard to present (sell) which is relatively simpler and faster for the executives to grasp.

Ideas typically get refined when people prepare to present. If you are responding to an RFP like an *Agile Follower*, you may be limited to iterate within specified parameters, in the hope to exceed customer expectations. If you are generating ideas and exploring markets at the same time like a *Smart Forecaster* or better. The sky is wide open for refinement.

---

[28] To Promote A New Idea, Forget the PowerPoint–Try A Billboard; Fast Company; Nov 30, 2012; https://www.fastcompany.com/3003484/promote-new-idea-forget-powerpoint-try-billboard

[29] Value Proposition Design; Alex Oseterwalder, Yves Pigneur, Greg Bernarda, and Alan Smith. Book, Wiley; 2014.

ISO 56007 Idea Management

> This standard[30] will provide guidelines for the management of ideas, the people who have them and the benefits they bring. It aims to address idea management at both the strategic and operational level through the culture and leadership of an organization, opportunity and risk management, problem solving, tools and methods for managing creativity and ideas.

The author is one of the many experts contributing to this standard. We cannot delve into the detail until the standard is officially published.

The Baileys Story

Let us quickly look at the story of Bailey's Irish cream[31] - an alcoholic beverage flavored with cream, cocoa, and Irish whiskey. The initial thought took about 30 seconds. In another 45 minutes the idea was formed. Baileys seems to like that. However, a decade of experience kicked in and delivered a great idea - dropping cream into Ireland's beloved whiskey. They mixed the two ingredients in the kitchen, tasted the result and it was certainly intriguing, but, quite awful. Undaunted, they threw in some sugar and it got better, but it still missed something. They went back to the store, searching the shelves for something else. They found their salvation in Cadbury's Powdered Drinking Chocolate and added it to the formula. It tasted really good. Not only this, but the cream seemed to have the effect of making the drink taste stronger, like full-strength spirit. It was extraordinary.

Names can be tough and often really easy to reject with a comment like *"I just don't like it."* Getting to Baileys as quickly as they did was unusual. Indeed, as they discovered in later years, it was incredible.

---

[30] To be Published in spring 2022.
[31] 9 Ways Bailey's Irish Cream Can Help You Innovate; Devin Mcintire; https://ideascale.com/9-way-baileys-irish-cream-can-help-you-innovate/ April 10, 2018.

The next step was the packaging, and they needed a bottle. They were not confident enough in the overall idea to spend money on a new mold. So, they looked around for an existing bottle and liked an Irish whiskey bottle of Redbreast. When Baileys finally had a potential bottle, label, and name, the team took it to a bar for some market research. They served it to a group of men who declared it to be a 'girly drink'. While it seemed like this could be a disaster for their new idea, they paid attention to all the feedback this group produced. But when they looked at their glasses every one of them had been drained. It might not have been their kind of drink, but there was nothing wrong with the taste. It was this keen observation that helped give the Bailey's team the confidence they needed to take their prototype to Dublin and present it to executives.

The lesson is that ideation does not end with the initial ideation session. It is a part of the entire innovation process, packaging, delivery, marketing, and even sustenance. Most of the ideation techniques and discussions in this chapter can be carried throughout the value stream and product life cycle.

Let's Summarize

Ideation, going beyond brainstorming, helps you ask the right questions and innovate with a strong focus on your users, their needs, and your insights about them. It goes a step beyond the obvious solutions and therefore increases the innovation potential of your solution. Ideation opens up unexpected areas of innovation by bringing together the perspectives and strengths of your team members. Facilitated sessions with carefully selected techniques and triggers create quantity, quality and variety in your innovation options, get obvious solutions out of your heads, and drive your team beyond them.

Let's Take a Selfie

 # I am guilty of reacting this way: *"That's a great idea, But …"*

- ☐ I don't think, our company will fund that!
- ☐ Let me play devil's advocate.
- ☐ You should talk to …
- ☐ Last time we attempted something like this, it was…
- ☐ Can you show me who has done it successfully?
- ☐ I won't buy this product.
- ☐ Can we discuss it in the staff meeting and see what others think?
- ☐ … and …
- ☐

 # We have the following in our organization:

- ☐ Facilitators for structured ideation.
- ☐ Creative room for ideation sessions.
- ☐ Techniques for structured ideation.
- ☐ Idea management software and repository.
- ☐ Mr. Anti-Idea Manager.
- ☐ Ms. Idea Robber.
- ☐ … and …
- ☐

4.   *Purposeful Qualification*

CHAMPIONS KEEP PLAYING, UNTIL THEY GET IT RIGHT
– BILLIE JEAN KING

For 2 years, I had the job of managing investments worth a few million-dollars in the development of advanced engineering design methods across a dozen managers. My biggest struggle was addressing the demand, that used to oversubscribe the capacity 4 times over. The best process we had was to remove the fat and redundancies, exploit synergies, prefer continuity, look at past performance, and future impact. We used a typical excel based approach to prioritize and down-select based on a return on investment calculation. It generally made good sense for incremental type projects with near-term returns. At that point of time, it appeared great and worked well enough to everyone's satisfaction. Today, I know better. I think that the process limited our ability to stretch our imagination, creativity, and probably eliminated what could have been breakthroughs. I wish I had better insight 15 years ago. Today, I see corporations still doing the same; and small businesses making decisions from the gut. This chapter can help all those organizations take good ideas one step closer to monetization.

Successful ideation and market insights are just the start. Most of the ideas go nowhere, because they need a passionate individual to drive through a process of qualification, iterative improvement, and implementation.

First, the idea must add value to someone whom we will call the user or customer. It should solve a problem, relieve pain, or provide gains that someone is willing to pay for. There needs to be a *Value Proposition*, which also fits your *Purpose*.

Second, it must make sense to your business. You should believe that you will be able to deliver it profitably, legally, and ethically, despite all its assumptions; before you invest your time and money to develop it. This faith-based milestone is called *Concept Qualification*, with full appreciation that the concept will still change as you discover new data and prove or disprove your assumptions.

Let us dig deeper into these steps.

Value Proposition

Strategyzer has made it simple for us though a canvas available in a book[32] and their website[33], also shown in the figure below. On the right side, you capture your customer's major Jobs-to-be-done, the pains in executing jobs today, and any gains they are willing to pay for when their job is done. The left side is about your offering, and how you can relieve the pain and create any gains for your customers.

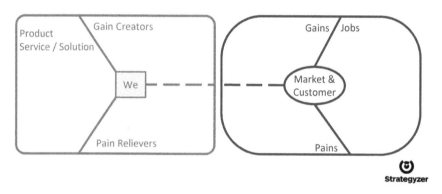

The boxes can be filled up in any sequence, with a few iterations to evolve until it all makes sense. You have to keep adjusting your Value Proposition (Ideas or a combination of ideas) based on the market insights (customer) to achieve solution-market fit. In the end you should be able to define it in one line.

---

[32] Value Proposition Design, Alex Oseterwalder, Yves Pigneur, Greg Bernarda, and Alan Smith; 2014.
[33] https://www.strategyzer.com/canvas/value-proposition-canvas

Purpose Check

Before spending any more effort on making a business case around the idea or Value Proposition, it is advisable to check and refine it in light of the purpose defined in Volume-1. What use would an idea be to acquire or launch a small technology business in Silicon Valley, if the purpose is to promote gender equality in Latin America?

If the concept is likely to create profits or sustain jobs, then it at least meets the basic purpose (Financial Drive). If there is a digital transformation somewhere, you are probably pushing technology (Industry 4.0) to solve a problem or addressing a social pull (Society 5.0)? I can understand that not everyone wants to save the ecosystem of our planet. I, however, urge you to check that your concept does not actively hurt humanity, society, or sustainability.

Sometimes you may be challenged to fit the value proposition with the purpose. It is great if it overshoots. For example, it serendipitously makes use of renewable energy (sustainability), while you were building a new school for the blind (social cause). However, on the other side of it, a poor fit does not mean that you compromise on your purpose. It just means that you go back and generate more ideas, look for other markets, and iterate on the value proposition.

> In general, if you compromise your purpose to fit an idea,
> in the name of the business case, you accept and admit that
> your purpose statement is just a marketing slogan.

Concept Qualification

The Concept Qualification Sheet

At this stage, we assume that your selected idea or value proposition fits your purpose. Now is the time to assess the financial viability of the concept so the purpose can be achieved sustainably. Once again, we take the help of the Strategyzer Business Model Canvas[34] as a starting point. Over years of application, we have modified it to the Concept Qualification Sheet. In its simplest form, you go about filling the twelve boxes in the sequence as numbered, answering a few simple questions, or selecting from the suggested options, discussed here as an initial guidance.

1. **What is your value proposition?** (a) New somewhat disruptive product that is first in the marketplace; improved product performance through an incremental innovation; product adapted for a new market with different requirements; better look and feel through design appeal,

---

[34] Business Model Generation; Alexander Osterwalder and Yves Pigneur; Book, Wiley; 2010.

packaging, user interface; price break from delivering a similar product at a lower price; (b) internal process efficiency providing cost and risk reduction, speed to market; professional and intellectual services such as advisory, training; maintenance and sustenance solutions; online, interactive, real-time services; emergency response; etc.

2. **What market segments are you going after?** (a) Mass market offering millions of general public consumers; (b) niche market of finite customers, where customization is important; (c) specific customer with a unique need; or (d) multiple diversified, segmented markets.

3. **What are the existing options with the customers today?** (a) No existing option offering you an opportunity to create a new need and command price and profits; (b) few options with a barrier to entry, creating new value, making room for yourself, and waking up competition; (c) many options, with virtually no barrier to entry, difficult to create a differentiated value, requiring a creative business model, competing on price, and treating cost as king.

4. **What is your competitive edge?** (a) Capital - IP or Know-how, rare skills and talent, rare physical or virtual assets, (b) excellence in execution through an effective cost structure, speed, or location; (c) branding or public relations (PR).

5. **What primary activities do you need to undertake?** (a) Research & Development, design & prototype validation, cyber-physical platform, network, or integration; (b) production requiring manufacturing sources, supply chain; (c) aftermarket service & support; (d) financing.

This is the correct time and place to check for Regulatory requirements so you can properly address resource requirement.

6. **What is your resource requirement?** (a) Physical laboratory facilities and equipment, IT infrastructure; (b) Intellectual Assets such as knowledge base, talent; (c) financial assets and reserves; (d) compliance requirements; (e) partnerships and joint ventures; (f) Safety and regulatory.

7. **What sales channels would you be using?** (a) Direct to the mass market with physical stores with advertising, sales and marketing department, and virtual stores; (b) Indirect to the mass market through

partner stores, wholesalers, social Media, piece in a bundle; (c) Niche and unique market through conferences, trade shows, seminars/workshops, personal network, and referrals; (d) Customer controlled through automated vending machines, and self-service kiosks.

8. **What is your pricing model?** (a) Deterministic - listed fixed price, listed fixed price with controllable discounts (time, place, quantity), listed price differently for different market segments, actual cost + fixed Fee, freemium model, Insurance type mode, subscription model; (b) Real-time pricing - list price, but negotiable, yield-driven for perishables, unlisted opportunistic pricing, auction model. Box 3 might put an upper limit on the list price.

9. **What are your costs & cost risks?** Box 5 & 6 determines the minimum possible. The costs include (a) One-time costs such as development and establishment, (b) Fixed costs independent of production & sales; (c) Unit costs from cost of producing and selling each piece, accounting for economies of scale, scope; (d) Value-driven costs; and (e) negotiable costs.

The risks of cost overrun comes from under-estimation of activity effort, unanticipated activities, or poor estimate of resource costs.

10. **How much capacity does the market have for your offering?** (a) Mass market is from population and could be in millions of customers for commodity type products requiring dependable supply chain; (b) Niche market of few users/customers requiring customization, where expertise/knowledge is the key; (c) Unique market of a few, working as a special order, making the relationship as key.

11. **What market share do you hope to capture?** Box 4 & 7 determine the maximum market you can capture. It also depends upon the stage of the business (launch, growth, or mature stage). Market share could grow by creating as you go or taking away from an incumbent.

The risks of not being able to capture market share come from the inability to generate interest, unanticipated competition, underestimated marketing effort, or poor estimate of market segment.

12. **When will you breakeven?** Now calculate the time frame or the sales quantity to start making profits. This defines your need for financial stability through breakeven point accounting for startup, launch, and marketing expenses.

Your answers to boxes 9 & 11 will help you estimate your breakeven point.

Learning to use the Concept Qualification Sheet

If you look at the canvas, you wonder why we had to jump all over. Of course, the sequence of questioning is important. Equally important is connectivity and dependence. Each box has a relationship with its neighbor. To respect that, we had to place them in the manner as presented. Looking at the entire canvas, the upper row of boxes is all about functional or execution, and the lower row is all about financial aspects. Each financial box is primarily related to the functional boxes just above.

To build a good Concept Qualification Sheet (CQS), simply start with the value proposition in box 1 and keep going to end up with breakeven point, just below, in box 12. Boxes 1 and 2 can come from the Value Proposition canvas discussed earlier. As you go through, you will have to make assumptions, research data, make selections, and even iterate halfway through. Make sure to list all assumptions made along the way. If you cannot decide on a number, you can pick a range with some level of confidence. This margin must decrease as you continue to iterate and do more research.

If the breakeven does not make a proper business case, think about where in the upper row you can make changes to adjust the equation in the lower row. You may end up going back to re-defining your value proposition. And that is OK, as long as you do not compromise on the purpose. At any point make sure you do not lose the connection across the boxes. At every change, you must ask if it affects anything in the neighboring box. Until you balance this out, you do not have a qualified concept.

In my 5 years of applying this to over a hundred value propositions, I have never had any team ever get it right the first time. Doing this for the first time is going to feel like jumping into the pool for the first time.

> You cannot learn swimming from a book or the YouTube.
> You have to immerse yourself in the pool water.

Here are some common mistakes, I would like for you to consciously avoid.

1. Filling the boxes in the order you understand rather than as numbered.
2. Writing it linearly on a page from top-down like an essay or a traditional business case, rather than appreciating the connectivity and dependence of neighboring boxes.
3. Ignoring the top row while filling out the bottom row.
4. Making up the numbers without any basis.
5. Choosing to take an unrealistic market share. Just because you love the idea, it does not mean you can capture all the market.

Generally, it takes a few iterations before it begins to make sense, with some unknown numbers. It is best done as a team of Subject Matter Experts, sales and marketing, and finance guys. Good ones take about 40-80 hours of effort over 2 weeks of research as a team.

Example: (1) An engineer comes up with a smart health monitor for (2) application in hospital as a market to (3) replace expensive bulky diagnostic machines, (4) offering speed, cost, and ease of use. (5) The product needs to be developed and certified, requiring (6) a team of talented engineers, software developers, test lab, and test subjects, and (7) sales force.

Working through the financial numbers, the startup realized that with a price point of $40K (8), an initial investment of $10M, and unit cost of $30K (9), they need to capture 50% of the market, selling 1000 pieces. That is a daunting task, requiring a lot more marketing and sales effort. As they put that additional cost into the equation for market capture, it did not converge to a valid business model.

Revising, the entire scenario, we came up with a new value proposition, shown within dark boxes.

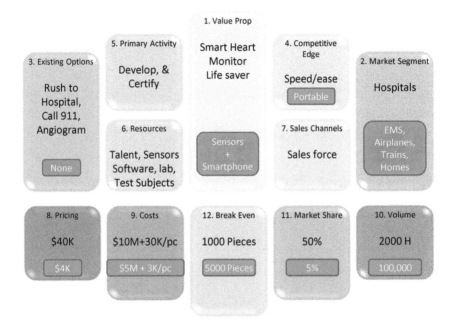

A combination of sensor suite and a smartphone makes a portable device going after a white space of emergency vehicles, airplanes, and trains, where there are no existing options. Suddenly the cost drops due to the smartphone use, market segments and market share goes up. Even at a much lower price point, the product can breakeven at a smaller market share (~5%) and that is quite doable, particularly in a white space.

Research and Validation in support of Concept Qualification Sheet

As discussed above, most of us will struggle with creating the concept qualification sheet in the beginning. Its simplicity is deceptive. You need to understand the current state of the art and the trends using a search across internal and external resources. If you find a lot of information, then you are probably looking at an older problem. If you find nothing, then you could be well ahead of your time. In today's context, there is a spurt of multi-disciplinary development. So, look across disciplines and domains to often find a wealth of knowledge in peripheral domains.

The information sources include …

- Company internal knowledge base of experience, and feedback.
- External published literature, government-funded projects, conferences.
- Information service providers with access to special databases.
- Experts in your network.

Once you get the data, or a range, and the concept appears to qualify, you should meet and review for dependability and confidence. It will not be accurate. However, with assumptions, it should still make good sense to kick-off a project. That is why it is called qualification.

At this point, it is good to address any barriers to your entry into the market as well as creating barriers to block the competition. This could make or break you in the long run. You must assume that there are bigger or more agile players in the market that can catch up with you and outperform quickly.

Leveraging the Concept Qualification Sheet

Take a scenario where, for a given objective, the team generated 84 ideas, later grouped under nine themes, leading up to nine value propositions. Each value proposition was assigned to the primary idea originator for concept qualification. Six of these nine concepts qualified. The leadership does not have enough funds to support all six of them. Here is how the sheet helps.

- Provide **side by side comparison** of activities, resources, uncertainty, markets, in addition to financial returns to help prioritize.
- Mix and match to **create a portfolio** of multiple projects to strike a balance across activities, resources, risks, and markets; and blend diverse projects with common elements.
- Put the unfunded projects **on hold** ready to go, whenever funds are available. Mark them with a shelf life, so that you review the assumptions again, lest they be no longer valid.

Process Concept Qualification Sheet

The concept qualification sheet for internal process innovation is slightly different.

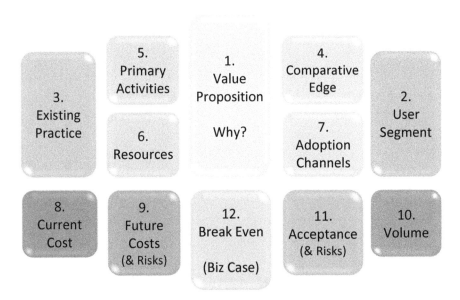

1. **What is your value proposition?** Proposal for internal process improvement, providing cost and risk reduction, speed to market, enhanced safety, etc.
2. **What user segments are you going after?** User group inside the company, and unless it will be sold or licensed out as a service, in which case use the service model discussed earlier.
3. **What is the existing practice today?** The current state of process execution.
4. **What comparative edge will the solution provide?** The additional value of the proposed process.
5. **What primary activities do you need to undertake?** (a) Research & Development, evaluation of commercially available options, (b) design & prototype validation; (c) Pilot implementation, transition, training, and adaption.
6. **What is your resource requirement?** (a) Physical laboratory facilities and equipment, IT infrastructure; (b) talent and other Intellectual Assets

such as knowledgebase; (c) financial assets and reserves; (d) compliance requirements; (e) partnerships and joint ventures; (f) safety and regulatory.

7. **What adaption channels would you be using?** How will this be sold to internal employees, for adaption? It could range from creating a pull or a push directive.

8. **What is the current cost per unit use?** Box 3 determines this.

9. **What is your future cost & cost risks?** Box 5 & 6 determine the minimum possible. The costs include (a) one-time costs such as development and establishment, (b) fixed costs independent of usage (c) unit costs for every use.

The risks of cost overrun comes from under-estimation of activity effort, unanticipated activities, or poor estimate of resource costs.

10. **How much usage do you expect for the new solution?** Current or projected workload on the system/process in terms of time or unit of a cycle.

11. **What acceptance share do you hope to capture?** For push-type it could be 80%. For pull it could be as low as 30-50% acceptance, while the rest continue to use the existing system. The risk is low and can be mitigated by the directive.

12. **When will you breakeven?** Now calculate the time frame and/or units of use to justify the investment. If the process innovation is based on technology that is rapidly changing, then the breakeven period should not be longer than expected obsolescence.

Your answers to boxes 8, 9 & 11 will help you estimate breakeven point. If the process improvement involves the industry 4.0 digital technologies, then breakeven point should account of obsolescence.

Amazon's Approach to Concept Qualification[35]

Ian McAllister, Director of Amazon Day shared an insightful look into Amazon's approach for product development on Quora a few years ago. The approach is known as 'working backwards' which begins by '[trying] to work backwards from the customer, rather than starting with an idea for a product and trying to bolt customers onto it.'

For a new initiative, a product manager must write an internal press release announcing a finished product, which might look like this:

Heading: Name the product in a way the reader (i.e., your target customers) will understand.

Subheading: Describe who the market for the product is and what benefit they get. One sentence only underneath the title.

Summary: Give a summary of the product and the benefit. Assume the reader will not read anything else so make this paragraph good.

Problem: Describe the problem your product solves.

Solution: Describe how your product elegantly solves the problem.

Quote from you: A quote from a spokesperson in your company.

How to get started: Describe how easy it is to get started.

Customer quote: Provide a quote from a hypothetical customer that describes how they experienced the benefit.

Closing and call to action: Wrap it up and give pointers where the reader should go next.

By working backwards, you get the chance to work on your idea and flesh it out. But you are also forced to put it to the test. After writing and rewriting, refining, and reiterating, it will become clear if the idea is worth pursuing. That clarity often helps you to let go of mediocre ideas so you can

---

[35] Amazon Uses a Secret Process for Launching New Ideas — and It Will Transform the Way You Work; Justin Bariso; Inc. Magazine; https://medium.com/inc/amazon-uses-a-secret-process-for-launching-new-ideas-and-it-will-transform-the-way-you-work-aec5c9121ae Dec 18, 2019.

concentrate on great ones. If the product makes it into development, the press release can then be used as a touchstone.

I have personally never used it. It appears closer to a Value Proposition than a Concept Qualification (business case). I am not sure if it can be used for quantitative side by side comparison or portfolio building. It certainly drives towards superior customer experience, which is one of the obsessions for Jeff Bezos.

Re-Innovate or Re-Purpose the Wheel (Mobile Devices)

By definition, a **wheel** is a circular component that is intended to rotate on an axle bearing. Wheels, in conjunction with axles, allow heavy objects to be moved easily facilitating transportation while supporting a load, or performing labor in machines. A wheel greatly reduces friction by facilitating motion by rolling together with the use of axles.

We do not reinvent the wheel. For ages, we have been re-innovating or re-purposing the wheel to solve new problems. E.g., the big inflatable wheel for beach application, a 3-small wheel configuration for the wheelchair that can be used to go over a curb, cog-wheel for trains on steep slopes, multiple wheels with a chain or belt around for battle tanks providing an all-terrain capability, Ferris wheel for amusement, flywheel to store potential energy (inertia), Pottery wheel, Steering wheel, Pully, Gears, fidget spinner, and many more.

In the 4th industrial revolution, **a mobile device is like a wheel**. Your smartphone has so much power in it, for so little cost. It offers Computing processor, Data storage and cloud connectivity, Audio Communication (Speaker, Mic), Video Communication (Display, Camera), Data Communication (Internet, Wi-Fi), Location services, and so much more.

I have found it quite useful to throw a cell phone into any new concept development as a component and build only what is required outside of it. It provides a significant added advantage that someone else is making these devices better every day; and you can focus on your core competency and application.

Some of my favorite questions are ...

1. Can you just go with a sensor suite and smartphone combination for your device rather than the full up box?
2. Can you think of integrating a cell phone as the system's user interface?
3. Have you thought of creating an app to go with your device?
4. Have you thought of engaging your users through their mobile devices?

I do this because, a good number of us do not think like that until we see it, or someone else tells us.

Ethics Check

Once you have defined the value proposition and the various steps in your Concept Qualification Sheet, you know enough about how to achieve it, and can do an early ethics check. A few simple starter questions are ...

- ☐ Is it the right thing for the customer, and any other affected parties?
- ☐ Is it the right thing for the business owners, and the employees?
- ☐ Is it the right way to do things?
- ☐ Can the product/service hurt the consumer, society, or the planet?

There is an area of real concern here when innovation happens faster than laws and regulations needed to keep the business drivers in check, and particularly where there is no precedence to provide initial guidance.

People innovating faster than law can keep up with

Who is watching out for us?

People making business decisions based on legal risk; The regulations are lagging

There is no precedence to learn from

There are serious questions about programming machines to replace human activity. Greg Satell says that when businesses gain access to advanced technologies like artificial intelligence and gene editing, the managers will be thrown into an unusual position. Should a self-driving car risk killing its passenger to save a pedestrian? Do decisions made by robots require greater transparency than those made by humans? Who gets to decide which factors are encoded into AI systems that make decisions about our education, whether we get hired or if we go to jail? How will these systems be trained? We all worry about who is educating our kids, who is teaching our algorithms? Powerful new genomics techniques like CRISPR (clustered regularly interspaced short palindromic repeats) open further ethical dilemmas. What are the guidelines for editing human genes? What are the risks of a mutation inserted in one species jumping to another? Should we revive extinct species, *Jurassic Park* style? What are the likely potential consequences? What is striking about the moral and ethical issues of both artificial intelligence and genomics is that they have no precedence. We are in a totally uncharted territory. Nevertheless, we must develop a consensus about what principles should be applied, in what contexts, and for what purposes.

> The topic is likely to be an endless debate,
> with continuously evolving perspectives.

As we move forward in Industry 4.0, we need to give serious thought to the responsibility of the agency. Who is responsible for the decisions a machine makes? What should guide those decisions? What recourse should those affected by a machine's decision have? These are no longer theoretical debates, but practical problems that need to be solved.

A good friend David Gilbert from the UK shared these ethical concerns with me, in terms of robotics and automation. Many robots use Artificial Intelligence and Machine Learning, which does not, of itself, create ethical issues, it can introduce ethical problems, from the redistribution of risk, where actions may have positive and negative effects on multiple individuals at the same time. The ability to oversee, or govern a robot is an ethical issue, as operators should be able to understand and manage the behavior of systems for which they are responsible. When the decisions are not transparent, i.e. open to scrutiny, there is a possibility that they are both unfair (unjust) and not open to correction. Robots might have a bias in their decision making (based on their learning). Robots may contain, and be able to provide to third parties, data that could violate an individual's right to privacy. Robots present the risk, especially to vulnerable users, of emotional attachment or dependency.

Another alarming area is the use of machine learning in e-commerce. Pricing algorithms have become ubiquitous in online retail. They have moved from rule-based programs to reinforcement-learning ones, where the logic of deciding a product's price is no longer within a human's control. A new paper[36] suggests that these systems could pose a huge problem: they quickly learn to collude, purely by trial and error, with no prior knowledge of the environment in which they operate, and without being specifically designed or instructed to collude." This leads to a risk of driving up the price of goods and ultimately harming consumers.

In May 2018, Franck et.al. published a paper[37] showing ethical consideration around e-cigarettes, touted as "better than tobacco". The abstract says:

> Due to their similarity to tobacco cigarettes, electronic cigarettes (e-cigarettes) could play an important role in tobacco harm reduction. However, the public health community remains divided concerning the appropriateness of endorsing a device whose safety and efficacy for smoking cessation remain unclear. We identified the major ethical considerations surrounding the use of e-cigarettes for tobacco harm reduction, including product safety, efficacy for smoking cessation and reduction, use among non-smokers, use among youth, marketing and advertisement, use in public places, renormalization of a smoking culture,

---

[36] Artificial intelligence, algorithmic pricing, and collusion; Emilio Calvano, Giacomo Calzolari, Vincenzo Denicolò, and Sergio Pastorello; 03 February 2019
https://voxeu.org/article/artificial-intelligence-algorithmic-pricing-and-collusion
[37] Ethical considerations of e-cigarette use for tobacco harm reduction; C. Franck, K B. Filion, J. Kimmelman, R. Grad, and M J. Eisenberg; Respir Res; pp17-53; 2016.

and market ownership. Overall, the safety profile of e-cigarettes is unlikely to warrant serious public health concerns, particularly given the known adverse health effects associated with tobacco cigarettes. As a result, it is unlikely that the population-level harms resulting from e-cigarette uptake among non-smokers would overshadow the public health gains obtained from tobacco harm reduction among current smokers. While the existence of a gateway effect for youth remains uncertain, e-cigarette use in this population should be discouraged. Similarly, marketing and advertisement should remain aligned with the degree of known product risk and should be targeted to current smokers. Overall, the available evidence supports the cautionary implementation of harm reduction interventions aimed at promoting e-cigarettes as attractive and competitive alternatives to cigarette smoking, while taking measures to protect vulnerable groups and individuals.

While you can argue that it a good alternate for smokers; but the manufacturers will be driven by business reasons to go after non-smokers, youth, and for use in public places as well, increasing the overall harmful effect on society.

In July 2019, a judge had ruled in a legal case brought by the American Academy of Pediatrics, American Heart Association, American Lung Association, and other medical groups that vaping companies have until May 2020 to have their products approved by the FDA. By Sept 2019, over 530 users of e-cigarettes had been struck with a vaping-related lung illness and 8 people had died from this affliction. The reports span 38 states and the U.S. Virgin Isles. The FDA and CDC began investigations into these lung illnesses resulting in a September 10 letter to Juul—a large manufacturer of e-cigarettes and cartridges—that they violated federal law by stating their product is 'safer' than other forms of tobacco. Walmart announced that it will cease selling vapers.

Another example from recent times is Boeing 787 MAX; wherein 2 crashes within 5 months killed 346 people. The Indonesian safety council faulted airplane design, certification, maintenance, and flight crew actions. The Ethiopian administration assigned blame to the aircraft's software design. The U.S. National Transportation Safety Board (NTSB) concluded that malfunctions resulted in multiple cockpit alerts that likely confused the flight crews. The U.S. House of Representatives criticized Boeing's *'culture of concealment'* during certification and in the aftermath of both accidents.

> There is something very wrong with your character,
> if the opportunity controls your loyalty. — Rana Bahadur

Data Projects

Rachel Thomas[38] has compiled a few questions that provide guidance when working with data projects. Have you …

☐ Listed how this technology can be attacked or abused?
☐ Tested your training data to ensure that it is fair and representative?
☐ Studied and understood possible sources of bias in your data?
☐ Included diversity of opinions, backgrounds, and kinds of thought?
☐ Set up a mechanism for gathering consent from users?
☐ Set up a mechanism for redress if people are harmed by the results?
☐ Created a safe shut down mechanism when it is behaving badly?
☐ Tested for fairness with respect to different user groups?
☐ Tested for disparate error rates among different user groups?
☐ Ways to monitor for model drift and ensure fairness over time?

With the social unrest going on in 2020 around racism, such issues will be center stage to acceptance of data driven technologies.

DoD's Ethical Principles for AI

The U.S. Department of Defense officially adopted a series of ethical principles[39] for the use of Artificial Intelligence on Feb 24, 2020 following recommendations provided to Secretary of Defense Dr. Mark T. Esper by the Defense Innovation Board in October 2019. These principles will apply

---

[38] 16 Things You Can Do to Make Tech More Ethical; Rachel Thomas; fast.ai; 22 Apr 2019; https://www.fast.ai/2019/04/22/ethics-action-1/
[39] DoD Adopts Ethical Principles for Artificial Intelligence; US DoD; Feb. 24, 2020. https://www.defense.gov/Newsroom/Releases/Release/Article/2091996

to both combat and non-combat functions and assist the U.S. military in upholding legal, ethical, and policy commitments in the field of AI. The department's AI ethical principles encompass five major areas:

Responsible*:* DoD personnel will exercise appropriate levels of judgment and care, while remaining responsible for the development, deployment, and use of AI capabilities.

Equitable*:* The Department will take deliberate steps to minimize unintended bias in AI capabilities.

Traceable*:* The Department's AI capabilities will be developed and deployed such that relevant personnel possess an appropriate understanding of the technology, development processes, and operational methods applicable to AI capabilities, including with transparent and auditable methodologies, data sources, and design procedure and documentation.

Reliable: The Department's AI capabilities will have explicit, well-defined uses, and the safety, security, and effectiveness of such capabilities will be subject to testing and assurance within those defined uses across their entire life-cycles.

Governable*:* The Department will design and engineer AI capabilities to fulfill their intended functions while possessing the ability to detect and avoid unintended consequences, and the ability to disengage or deactivate deployed systems that demonstrate unintended behavior.

These principles can be adopted in the commercial sector, since these recommendations came after 15 months of consultation with leading AI experts in commercial industry, government, and academia. The development team followed a rigorous process of feedback and analysis among the nation's leading AI experts with multiple venues for public input and comment.

Let's Summarize

Out of dozens of clients in the last 6 years, this concept qualification method has been the single most popular and eye-opener process; because

- The idea originator loves to get multi-disciplinary support, is better prepared and more confident presenting it to the leadership for sponsorship.
- The leadership loves to see it all on one page, and together they can tweak it to mutual satisfaction.
- The ones that get funded are happy. The ones that did not, know why not, and can do better next time. Their faith in the process makes rejection more palatable.
- It makes it easier to track deviation from what was originally approved.
- I have also heard from customers that it has helped them rebuild team spirit, even across departments.
- *Most importantly*, it significantly reduces leadership bias, and emotional decision making, through the process, data, and transparency. This may sometimes make the middle management a little uncomfortable.
- It will be a great day, when ethics built into the system will stop unethical people from harming the society. The story of twitter bots[40] spreading misinformation about the pandemic on social media and pushing America to reopen is quite disturbing.

---

[40] Nearly half of Twitter accounts pushing to reopen America may be bots; Karen Hao, May 21, 2020; https://www-technologyreview-com.cdn.ampproject.org/c/s/www.technologyreview.com/2020/05/21/1002105/covid-bot-twitter-accounts-push-to-reopen-america/amp/

Let's Take a Selfie

 # Let me look at what's new for us from this chapter.

My current process	Value Proposition + Concept Qualification

 # Our Principles or Ethics checks include ...

5.   *Creative Execution*

NOBODY CARES ABOUT YOUR IDEAS, UNTIL IT BECOMES REALITY
– AFRA SANJARI

In 1985, as an Aeronautical Engineering senior, I once got into a discussion with my professor on design projects. He politely explained to me how the students are minimalist and do not want to work any harder than they need to. Remember, my father had always encouraged me to go above and beyond and challenge the status quo. I went to our department head Prof. Malhotra and expressed my desire to design and build *something*. He supported me, somewhat hesitantly, offering me help with the design, but not with the fabrication. He was kind enough to arrange a nitrocellulose-nitroglycerin cartridge and suggested that I design a rocket engine around that. I got a couple of my friends excited into building a rocket-propelled model of a missile.

Our design was a foot-long steel body, with a 3.5 Mach exit gas velocity, which required a convergent-divergent supersonic nozzle. The cartridge would burn for less than a second and propel the missile model to carry it over 3 miles. In the very first design discussion with the faculty, they asked us to cut down the range to 100m so we could test it within our sports grounds and not have to worry about air space violations. That made the design much simpler, weight was no longer a consideration. We could take a mild steel rod and drill an axial hole for the cartridge and put in the nozzle at the other end. We discovered that the cartridge was 1.1" in diameter and the biggest drill bit in the college workshop was 1.0". We had no money to buy anything. The college refused to buy a new drill bit.

We started brainstorming and came up with a crude way of doing it. Stick in a small piece of wire between the drill bit and the drill chuck, to hold it eccentrically[41]. We choose not to discuss this hack with anyone in the workshop and went to the lathe machine. We got the hole we needed. Recall the story of drill machine and the hole. We were focused on the hole.

nce the rocket was assembled, we decided to test it by holding it in a vice on the workbench inside the workshop. The test failed. Turned out that there was not enough charge in the igniter to create a uniform starter burn. We redesigned the ignitor and ran the test a second time. This time, the exhaust blast was powerful enough to slam the door shut 10 feet away. We were happy and excited to go to the field. The following day, it dawned on us how lucky we were not to have been in the exhaust's wake. The concept of personal protective equipment was alien to us back then. The news quickly spread about a successful lab test, younger students gravitated to the

toy and we had to start securing our assets at the end of every day. The professors were excited as well.

We built a small portable launch pad, redid the range/height calculation, and tested it in the field. This time we were all standing far enough. The first attempt was a vertical launch, and the model rose to about the estimated height, fell back, and broke the nose cone as well as the stabilizing fins. With a new set of parts, our next launch was at a 45° angle for maximum range. We hit the target 110m away, that was almost 10x10 meter in size, deliberately chosen to be large enough. We all learned a lot - creativity, agility, persistence, teamwork, limitations, and the power of clearly defined objectives. Our teammate Dr. Jatinder Singh now heads a division of National Aerospace Labs in India. Our other team member Group Captain Aurobindo Handa heads the Aircraft Accident Investigation Board in India.

Ideas are necessary, but not sufficient. Execution is what makes the difference. Every time I see SpaceX and Elon Musk, I feel *"Now that is a real deal. I was only making toys."*

---

[41] Please don't try this at home or at work place.

Defining the Innovation Project

Once the concept is qualified and funded, the real task of project management begins. It is not my intent to rewrite a project management manual, but I feel that if I do not put this in the context of uncertainty associated with innovation, this book will be incomplete.

Define Success Criterion

Start with the value proposition and define the shape of the project when successful – qualitative or quantitative (preferred). Ensure that it is still aligned with your purpose, and the objectives of your financial sponsor (or the customer intent). Defining a success criterion is not always as black and white as hitting a target. And at times, it makes sense to have shades of gray in between. Most projects and activities these days are team efforts, and you are faced with diverse perspectives, and opinions. This diversity combined with uncertainty calls for the need to document successes. I know of executives who deliberately choose not to define success criteria, so they can declare a successful outcome at the end of the project (an unethical approach in my world).

Agile Followers usually define the quantitative success criterion for the end. *Smart Forecasters* typically define success criterion as a combination of quantitative and qualitative outcomes with an occasional need for an intermediate step.
Visionary Trendsetters generally define success criteria for the next stage in a multistage project, with a vision for the final outcome, which also evolves with learning.

Develop Requirements Documents

Once again, the best way to address assumptions, uncertainties, risks, and changes associated with an innovation project, is to document whatever you need to accomplish at product, system, or subsystems level. Some assumptions made during the concept qualification, will not come true. They will require revisiting the business case, to ideate on alternate paths, and to pivot a few times to be successful.

This is also the time to identify all compliance requirements - industry standards, government regulations, certifications, and approvals. Venturing into new areas, may require having to work with a new government organization. Every medical device startup investment begs an FDA question. I know of a startup that changed its objectives from human-drug to pet-drug just to secure venture capitalists (financial purpose), who do not want to deal with the regulators. How sad!

Agile Followers document requirements to meet customer expectations.
Smart Forecasters create documents to manage internal expectations.
Visionary Trendsetters are generally poor at documentation. Sketches and Microsoft Office files are a common occurrence at start, until a project is formulated.

Build the Team

This is the most difficult part and makes a big difference. That is why investors pay close attention to the startup team and not just the idea. Smart organization leaders go for the passion in the idea originator, for anything visionary. A common mistake in building a new product development team is the realization of important roles.

Team for Process Innovation: This team needs the individuals involved in the current process to start with. Now bring in someone with a good grasp of the technology or solution being brought in. With industry 4.0, expertise in Information and Communication Technology (ICT) is a must, whether it is AI, IoT, 3D Printing, … I also suggest bringing along the finance manager and the talent development manager[42] in this case. Finance ought to understand heavy investment upfront and perhaps think about a

---

[42] Talent development manager is a specific role for individual and team development focused on training and mentoring, sometimes handled well by HR.

phased investment to make it all affordable. The talent development manager ought to consider training programs to re-skill the staff.

Team for Product Innovation: This team ought to start with the individuals who first came up with the idea at the core. Remember, idea originator always has an advantage. Now you need to bring in individuals to cover all these aspects: (1) Design and development process, (2) Discipline expertise and cross-discipline interactions, (3) Domain and market knowledge, (4) Understanding of product life cycle from conception to aftermarket support, (5) Appreciation of the business case and business risk, (6) project and people management, and (7) Finance and talent development manager if required. I have realized that it is very helpful to engage your end-user or customer or have someone role-play that in the team throughout the development process.

Team for Business Model Innovation: This team is more around skills with market domain, buyer persona, human psychology, sociology, finance, and marketing to support the idea originator. If it is a significant departure from the current business model, C-suite ought to be involved.

Team Diversity and Dynamics: Building a team is more than picking the right set of skills and individuals. Team lead has to make them work together, to a point where the whole is more than the sum of individuals. To be truly innovative, teams should try to include different cognitive styles. According to Anita Williams Woolley[43], of Carnegie Mellon University, too little diversity stagnates, while too much diversity creates hard to bridge gaps. The study labeled participants according to three different cognitive styles: verbalizers, spatial visualizers, and object visualizers, which describe how people receive and analyze information. Journalists and lawyers tend to be verbalizers; engineers and people in other math-driven professions are spatial visualizers, who think analytically; and artists are object visualizers, who tend to think about the bigger picture. You can design teams to be

---

[43] The Impact of Cognitive Style Diversity on Implicit Learning in Teams; Ishani Aggarwal, Anita Williams Woolley, Christopher F. Chabris, & Thomas W. Malone; Frontiers in Psychology, Feb 2019.

collectively intelligent, and that lays the groundwork for them to perform well and adapt when circumstances change.

Over the last 6 years, every time we successfully clarified such roles and assigned unique responsibilities on the project teams, held team-building exercises, and happy hours, we noticed more creativity and less conflicts. It also accelerated innovation, built stronger and longer-lasting teams which quickly gained leadership confidence for additional funds.

Establish the Review Structure

An equally important item in projects with a high degree of uncertainty, is a process to periodically review progress, address assumptions, review risks, assure quality and compliance, monitor investment, address talent gaps, and pivot as new knowledge emerges. The traditional phase-gate process is enough, but it needs to be executed at the right cadence and with rigor, judicious tolerance to risk, and still provide encouragement to the team. The subsequent sections on managing risk go into further details on this.

Managing Execution Risk

Significance of Review Gates

A quick story to illustrate the point. After a nasty accident at an intersection, city authorities asked *"Why do we not have a STOP sign here?"* Reply came back as *"People were complaining about seconds lost due to "stop and go" on an intersection with virtually no traffic. Since we have not had an accident here in a long time, we took the sign off, just yesterday."* There is a reason for a 4-way stop sign. Stop and look for what is coming from the side?

For Business Leaders: Annual or quarterly strategic reviews serve this purpose, to pause and look for where the competitor might be coming from. All it takes is a little time with the Board of Directors to properly re-position for success.

For Innovation Managers: A review gate with a pre-defined success criterion is a recognized best practice. All it takes is a little time with a group of experts to mitigate risk and quality concerns, and redirect for success.

Gates: Generically speaking, qualified concepts that proceed to become projects may go through these gates:

- Proof of Concept.
- Product/service design and development.
- Performance verification and validation.
- Pilot users and customers.
- Scale-up and capture market share.

Depending upon complexity, confidence, and risk assessment, the project may have more or fewer gates. A simple study project may have an interim content review and final report and review. Complex product design may have a hierarchical gate structure such as component design gate(s) to support a system-level design gate. A very popular example of a gated process is the Technology Readiness Levels used by DoD/NASA and many other commercial organizations. A similar one called Manufacturing Readiness Levels is used by many organizations.

> The phase-gate process is to minimize cost and risk of innovation project through synergy and alignment of expectations.

The process ...

- Defines the review team, and lays out the GO/NO-GO criteria upfront.
- Provides a forum and timing to discuss and approve any scope changes.
- Clarifies and adapts the roles & responsibilities during execution.
- Facilitates informed decision making for the continuation of the project based on the availability of resources, business case, and risk analysis.

The outcome of each review gate could be categorized under various classes:

- **GO** with comments or recommendations for the next phase.

- **Conditional GO** with specific actions by a date for it to be a GO.
- **NO-GO – RE-DO** with required actions and return for review.
- **NO-GO – HOLD** with specific unmet criteria, or changed context; and a temporary hold of the project, for a specific period.

A project should only move forward to the next review gate, when both the product/service development and business development feel that the concept still qualifies; and all the previous gated criteria have been successfully met. Any exception to the review gate or waiver of criteria/ expectations should require a review team approval. The higher the uncertainty, the lower the first pass yield.

With some of my clients, I notice a management metric around increasing the first pass yield of gated reviews. That is not a good practice. It drives many wrong behaviors: (a) a tendency to pick low-risk ideas/projects, (b) to keep working to perfection, and (c) the review team's bias towards a 'GO' outcome. That is all counter to innovation and the purpose of a gated review. We want to fail fast and learn fast. It is OK to track, but do not set a goal for yield.

Agile Followers usually have a high success rate generally ending as 'Conditional GO' often characterized by schedule and cost pressure on low uncertainty projects.

Smart Forecasters typically have a moderate success rate and a few 'RE-DO'.

Visionary Trendsetters explore hard and broad and are OK with low yield and lessons through 'RE-DO' or 'NO-GO.'

Review Gate Team

Having worked at a major aerospace manufacturer, I had the good fortune of being a part of several reviews at various levels and disciplines – design, technology, component, system, product, manufacturing, process, program, and so on. That process was so mature, that I did not realize what a poor process feels like until I was assigned to develop suppliers. Now having coached over 2 dozen product innovation companies on this topic, I can confidently say that the value of review gates comes from a competent and empowered review team. The review team must be competent to make the right decisions and mentor the team. It must be empowered to judge and stop/redirect a project, despite business pressures.

The suggested participation for the project review team under phase-gate process includes these ...

- Funding sponsors, who are accountable for profit & loss.
- Product/service line heads, who will eventually own this innovation.
- New Business Development, which has to generate revenue from this.
- The project team, to defend the progress and learn from gate experience.
- Chiefs or subject experts, who are responsible for technical excellence.
- Optional invitees, such as retirees, Consultants, or Customers, for wisdom.

The team needs to maintain a healthy level of conflict and collaboration at the same time amongst various roles/disciplines. For example:

- The marketing and development folks should collaborate throughout to work toward the same innovation and timeline.
- Talent development manager and innovation chief should collaborate for proper talent acquisition and development.
- Program manager and Subject Matter Experts could have a conflict all the time for product excellence and project cost/schedule performance.
- Market domain experts and Subject Matter Experts have a conflict or collaborative depending upon customer push and pull for innovation.

Having seen so many reviews with passionate debates, leading to some exciting outcomes, I say *"conflict at the review gate is a good thing."* How we choose to resolve that conflict during the review or afterward as an action item, defines the review gate experience and employee engagement with innovation. The team ought to go into the gate review with an open mind, focused on the purpose, objectives, ethics, and educating each other. In the end, both the project and the review teams are all on the same side, fighting uncertainty.

False Calls at the Review Gate

The purpose of a review gate is to reduce the risk, by ensuring continuation as long as the concept still qualifies. The review team is susceptible to human errors, misjudgment, and decision making with limited information, cost and schedule constraints, or sometimes external pressures.

A true positive (GO when it should have been a GO) ensures progress, confidence, and team buy in.

A true negative (RE-DO when it should have been a RE-DO) improves learning, saves failure later reducing losses, builds stronger teams, and drives humility.

A false negative (RE-DO when it should have been a GO) leads to some unnecessary rework, schedule delays, and a demoralized team when they are confident. The positive that comes out is improved communication.

A false positive (GO when it should have been a RE-DO or a NO-GO) will continue to accumulate losses and even an escape of a poor design to the market leading to liabilities. They usually make good learning stories, which drive process improvements, policies, and even regulations. Both Space Shuttle disasters were calls made under schedule pressure. The case of Boeing 737 Max software shortfall is a review process failure, which is supposed to look at every aspect of "continued operation".

Alternate Approach – 6 Thinking Hats[44]

Another approach to disciplined execution is by looking at the project or review gates from different perspectives. The challenge would be trying to juggle many things at once. The Six Hats allow us to systematically focus on different aspects of a situation or decision, to become more focused yet see a more complete picture. In some sense it is like looking at a dice by spinning it all around and concentrating on one face at a time.

---

[44] Six Thinking Hats, Edward de Bono; Book; 2015.

The white hat is for putting up facts and figures in a neutral and objective way, looking at available information, any gaps, and trends.

The red hat represents the emotional view, recognizing feelings, intuition, and gut reaction as an important part of thinking.

The black hat represents caution and identification of what could go wrong, recognizing the value of caution and risk assessment; to make the plans more robust.

The yellow hat focuses on value, benefits, and optimism, constructively driving returns on investment.

The green hat is about creativity, new ideas, and change, discovering new ideas, possibilities, and modifications.

The blue hat is for process control, and for managing and organizing thinking. It has a strategic role and helps to organize the other hats, assess priorities, list constraints etc. Unlike the other hats, the blue hat is a permanent role. It is worn by the facilitator or chairperson.

This exercise can be easily gamified by having these hats as physical props, brought in a review meeting, and assigned to various people. In the middle they can be rotated to get diverse inputs. I have personally never used this; else I would have had a story to tell.

Managing Market Risk

This is the final step in the innovative thought process to bring the cash in. Many ideas fail in the marketplace, even if they come from leading innovators such as Google or Amazon. Consider using the market insight to ideate for everything around customer experience – packaging, delivery, pricing, support, and now gamification.

Early Market Engagement

Although the qualified concept is holistic, it is a bunch of ideas, assumptions, and some data. It is pretty much all invention and creativity. Taking it to the market to create value for consumers and to generate revenue will potentially make it an innovation. You need to work through various aspects for it to be sticky in the marketplace. Let us look at some important ones for the sake of completeness, which should be considered during the review gates.

The product delivery model includes, packing, shipping, handling, setup, training, etc. and all that happens between the product leaving the manufacturer/retailer and buyer using it. Service delivery is a lot about transactional experience, communication, ambiance, and handling of an unhappy customer.

Business model is about setting the price, payment terms and billing, sell vs lease vs subscription, financing options, warranties, returns, trial period, bundling, and now mobile engagement…

Market positioning is making the customer think about your product through advertisements and social media. Naming and tag lines are probably the difficult ones, but have significant impact.

Market testing is when the manufacturer/developer wants to get an early indication of how the product or service will be received and accepted by the end-user. It might include focus groups, beta tester, pilot programs, and even up to the first few customers providing feedback.

As an innovator, we must also think of how to support the product in service and at the end of its useful life. What are the possible business models, in terms of ability to service, recycle, salvage? …

Product Packaging for Consumer Engagement

Packaging is no longer just a box. Almost every consumer product invests heavily in innovation in packaging. There are so many examples of packaging innovation to capture market share. Toothpaste companies reduced vanity shelf space by making broad caps and going standup mode. Pomegranate and lemon juice are packaged in bottles that look just like the fruit by shape and color to make it easily recognizable and to give the feel of the real thing. Plastic water bottles are shaped to reduce plastic materials and handling. Ketchup caps and nozzles were designed so that they do not drip. The box for Amazon Kindle oasis and Google Pixel Buds double up as chargers. Cardboard box for a 12-can-pack went from 4x3 to a 6x2 for ease of stacking in the refrigerator, and then a designer cut to create a dispenser. Many small electronic products use packaging to act as transportation, handling, shelf display, marketing, ... purposes as well.

Service Delivery for Customer Experience

The service industry is highly competitive as well. Coffee shops, aircraft interior, sports bars, amusement parks, holiday resorts, etc. go all out to make the experience memorable for you. They are all very innovative about creating customer experience through novelty, thrill, comfort, ambiance, security, safety, sanitization, etc. which are all of value to consumers.

Gamification for Consumer and Employee Engagement

Think about how to turn your service or product into a game-like experience. It is easier said than done. In product design and development, we can focus on user needs and goals to deliver meaningful experiences people value. Every goal has a motivation, and the key is to develop ways to help motivate people to reach their goals. What better way to motivate people than in a way that is engaging, rewarding, grounded in behavioral science, and even a little bit of fun for them to learn, explore, and use? All the while continuously giving them reasons to engage with your product. The five principles of gamification are ...

1. **Autonomy:** Urge to direct our own lives (I want to control).
2. **Mastery:** Desire to get better (I want to improve).
3. **Purpose**: Yearning to be a part of something larger than ourselves (I want to make a difference).
4. **Progress:** Desire to see results associated with mastery and purpose (I want to achieve).
5. **Social Interaction:** Need to belong, be connected to, recognized by, and interact with others (I want to engage others).

Take eBay as a prime example. Buyers and sellers rate each other. The more they buy, sell, and accumulate good ratings on the platform, the higher they rank in the community. Their ranking is represented with *status flair*, i.e. *Power Seller*, *Trusted Seller* etc., on their profiles and listings to build marketplace prominence and garner buyer and seller confidence.

Haven't we all fallen for frequent flyer miles or hotel rewards program? For five years, I tracked my actual flight costs based on the cheapest flights versus the Delta Amex equivalent. I came out ahead. Of course, the way out would be to have a frequent flyer card for every airline and use it after selecting the cheapest flight, but then it takes forever to accumulate enough useable miles on any airline. So, I do not fall for their game, anymore.

Uncertainty and Risk

We have talked about managing risk, without actually defining it or providing a tool to quantify easily. Here is something simple and useful, even if you know the subject well.

> According to ISO, **uncertainty** is defined as 'state of deficiency of information, understanding or knowledge.' The deficiency can be full or partial. Uncertainty can be related to the consequences, or likelihood of an event, or the characteristics of an entity. Uncertainties can be managed by systematically addressing critical assumptions regarding consequences, likelihood or characteristics of events and entities, to gain information, understanding and knowledge. (ISO56000:2020 Clause 3.2.6)

> According to ISO, **risk** is defined as 'effect of uncertainty.' An effect is a deviation from the expected — positive or negative. Risk is often characterized by reference to potential 'events' and 'consequences' or a combination of these. Risk is often expressed in terms of a combination of the 'consequences' of an event and the associated 'likelihood' of occurrence (ISO56000:2020 Clause 3.2.7)

Based on my years of efforts reducing risk in aviation, having learned from major airplane manufacturers, there is a third dimension to risk and that is related to early warning or indication that may provide adequate opportunity to avoid the event or contain the consequence. Thus, a practical approach is to qualitatively judge the risk using three parameters …

Likelihood: 1-Unlikely, 2-Possible, 3-Likely, 4-Probable, 5-Most likely.

Consequence: 1-Insignificant, 2-Noticeable, 3-Moderate, 4-Significant, 5-Severe.

Prevention opportunity: 0-Error proof, 1-Active safety, 2-Passive Safety or early warning, 3-Post event reporting, 4-No warning/report at all.

The product of these 3 numbers provides Risk Index on a scale of 0-100.

Risk Index = (Likelihood) x (Consequence) x (Prevention opportunity).

Based on the Risk index, the risk is classified, with suggested decision as … .

49-100: Serious. STOP. Reduce risk before proceeding further.

19-48: High. Prioritize risk mitigation actions, with confidence in the plan.

5-18: Medium. Have an approved risk mitigation plan.

1-4: Low. Be aware and keep improving.

0: None. Go back and verify the mistake-proofing steps.

If you notice, in the absence of any meaningful data, the process is subject to individual judgment. Usually a team effort provides a fairly good outcome. It certainly helps identify most of the risks, prioritize them, and take actions required to mitigate. In a good gate review process, every identified risk is quantified and addressed.

> When critical questions during a review process begin to identify new risks, then you know that the review process is working.

Let's Summarize

The only item worthy of special attention during innovation execution is risk and uncertainty management. Focus on an honest review at every stage-gate conducted by a competent and empowered team, followed by a pivot, if required. Do not marry the original idea. Most successful innovation outcomes look different than initially thought of.

Let's Take a Selfie

 # Two new things that I learned from this chapter are ...

6. *Variations in Innovation Value Chain*

WHEN YOU KNOW WHAT YOU WANT, AND YOU WANT IT BAD ENOUGH,
YOU'LL FIND A WAY TO GET IT
— JIM ROHN

During my early years of practice, we got called into a situation, where the client needed to come up with a strategy immediately to save their business unit from shutting down. We had less than a month to present a set of plausible options for turnaround. We purpose-built a small team of individuals and locked ourselves in an empty office away from the primary business location. The team members were handpicked to include strong direct product know-how, a sales guy, a startup co-founder, an engineering student, an arts student, a pilot, an emergency room nurse, and a business model specialist from a local incubator. They were all together in one building for 16 working days, were well fed, and enjoyed quality time bonding over happy hours. Ideas started flowing at an incredible rate around day 2, as the team members bonded around a common purpose. We followed the value chain in an accelerated manner to develop over 70 ideas, a dozen value propositions, and eventually six qualified concepts across various forms of innovation, such as …

1. Repackaged product for an adjacent market (Eco-adaptive) in 3 months.
2. Modified product for an existing market (Evolutionary) in 6-9 months.
3. A few accessories (Peripheral) for value-add in 9-12 months.
4. Derivative product for the emerging economy (Eco-adaptive) in 1 year.
5. Smart-product (Breakthrough) for the exiting market in 3-4 years.
6. Innovative business model through existing consumer consolidation.

The business unit is still in business, despite some initial discomfort at our recommendations. We called this exercise as **Burst Innovation Event.** The approach can also be used for the identification of a single new product or service solution. Almost a year later, I witnessed a similar story related to another leader through the eyes of an overseas customer. The leader maintains a list of *'Special Intellectual Forces'* to solve serious problems. When required, he would handpick a few, bring them into a hotel, provide a charter and resources, and motivate them to resolve the situation before they are permitted to go back home to their families.

At the Core of Innovation Process

At the core, most innovations are matchmaking between a problem and an idea. Market insight manifests as a 'problem' and ideation produces multiple possibilities to solve that 'problem'. Either one of them could come up first and look for its mate. The intermediate elements in the matchmaking process are Value Proposition, Concept Qualification, Purpose & Ethics check. The details of each of these process elements are different depending upon the Purpose and Profile characteristics.

In this chapter, we will cover the key characteristics and key process elements of various innovation types introduced in Chapter-1. Text with a ~~strike-through font~~ for Purpose and Profile indicates when that innovation type is rarely applicable.

Evolutionary Innovation

Key Characteristics

Objective: Retain or grow the market share through incremental improvement of the existing product or service for the existing market, typically.

Purpose: Financial, Technical, Social, Sustainability.

Profiles: Agile Follower, Smart Forecaster, Visionary Trendsetter.

Key Process Elements

Market is mostly the same where existing product is currently sold.

Customer insight is either easily available through simple VOC or easily predictable through simple linear extrapolation.

Ideation happens around the usage of existing product or customer feedback.

Value Proposition is relatively simple to create since the pains and gains do not need much debate.

Purpose Check is usually not required.

Concept Qualification has a lot of certainty due to the known product & market.

Phase-gate approach works quickly, effectively, and efficiently because the risks are generally low and easily understood.

Control of cost and speed to market is an important factor, because the competition is direct and predictable.

Example – New year, New Model

Most innovations that you see in everyday products, such as automobiles, appliances, furniture, garments, consumer electronics, gadgets, home improvement, and tools fit this category. Year over year you get newer models with improved features and conveniences.

Eco-adaptive Innovation

Key Characteristics

Objective: Capture new markets by adapting product/service to meet requirements specific to the new market.

Purpose: Financial, ~~Technical~~, Social, Sustainability.

Profiles: ~~Agile Follower~~, Smart Forecaster, Visionary Trendsetter.

Key Process Elements

Market is mostly new with slightly different set of requirements, or adaption nuances.

Customer insight is a significant component and needs an effort by people who understand the local market and consumer behavior.

Ideation is required around the intersection of new customer insights with the existing product.

Value Proposition requires a check on proper appreciation of new pains and gains of the new customer, which may be different than those used to create the baseline product.

Purpose Check will help understand if the business growth is into the right market domain, or geographical region for you; as well as product acceptance in a new market.

Concept Qualification has some uncertainty around the new market size.

Phase-gate approach needs to focus on market characteristics more than the product.

Example – Refrigerator Taking the Heat

Sometime in the 1990s a US appliance company introduced a high-tech frost-free refrigerator in the Indian market. It became quite a status symbol due to the price tag and brand name. Many of my rich neighbors and friends bought it very quickly. Within the year, we started hearing very similar breakdown stories and getting parts replaced under warranty. The challenge – the manufacturer did not adapt the machine to the Indian environment. Room temperatures were much higher in summer, because of no air conditioning, overloading the compressor. The Voltage fluctuations and power outages were taking a toll on the controls. The dust was settling on the coil at the bottom. The manufacturer realized this and changed the design – adapting to the Indian environment.

Peripheral Innovation

Key Characteristics

Objective: Generate additional revenue from the same market through adjacent or peripheral products/services, which add value to the primary product/service.

Purpose: Financial, Technical, Social, ~~Sustainability.~~

Profiles: Agile Follower, Smart Forecaster, ~~Visionary Trendsetter.~~

Key Process Elements

Market is mostly the same where the primary product is sold.

Customer insight is an important component in terms of needs, expectations, and willingness to go for more than a basic product.

Ideation is required around the intersection of new customer insight with the existing product.

Value Proposition requires a check on proper appreciation of new pains and gains of the customer, which may be different than those used to create the baseline product.

Purpose Check is usually not required.

Concept Qualification has little to no uncertainty and makes for a simple decision.

Phase-gate approach is simple and effective, focused on adding value, reducing risks, and is often around costs.

Example – GoPro gets hyperactive

Between 2010 to 2015, GoPro achieved five years of 90 percent average annual sales growth. The company added a smartphone app, a variety of camera mounts, desktop software to turn raw footage into polished movies, and a social media site for customers to share their adventures, in addition to the rugged, waterproof action camera. By 'dating their customer' GoPro was able to understand what the customers wanted to achieve with their cameras and to provide the complementary products and services to help them. Sony had a better and cheaper camera, but GoPro had a portfolio of complementary products and services that together helped customers capture their adventures.

Example – Lego Rediscovers new Blocks

After 15 straight years of 14 percent average annual growth, sales plateaued. Lego executives convinced themselves they had to overhaul their business, move away from their iconic brick, and reinvent the future of play before a competitor did. The result was four years of expensive failures. The company almost went bankrupt. But Lego learned a lesson: when it went away from the brick, customers had no reason to purchase Lego toys. While it wasn't sufficient to offer only a box of bricks, it was necessary. When Lego went back to the brick and innovated around it, customers returned to the brand, and the sales rebounded. To pursue this way, a company must start by defining the product or service it wants to innovate around, then decide its business promise to its customers, then design and deliver those complementary innovations to the market.

Lego checked all of those boxes when it introduced Lego Batman in 2006. A major movie followed in 2017. Along with Lego Batman, there were a series of complementary products designed to increase kids' involvement with the story. There was a comic book, happy meal toys, a video game, and an iPhone tie-in.

Crisis Innovation

Key Characteristics

Objective: Extremely rapid innovation to save human lives in jeopardy, with whatever resources are accessible. Cost is usually not a concern.

Purpose: ~~Financial~~, ~~Technical~~, Social, ~~Sustainability~~.

Profiles[45]: Agile Follower, ~~Smart Forecaster~~, ~~Visionary Trendsetter~~.

Key Process Elements

Market is the few humans and their families; whose lives are in jeopardy.

Customer insight is about rapid & continuous situational awareness and assessment. This can vary from nothing to full and 2-way communication depending upon the situation.

---

[45] If we dig deeper, we may discover that successful Crisis Innovation deserves a profile of its own, however in context of the profile definitions, innovating in response to a need is a "Follower".

Ideation is the key component, needs to be rapid, exhaustive, but constrained by accessible resources (people, tools, materials, energy, mobility, devices, MedTech).

Value Proposition is clear, and generally requires no discussion.

Purpose Check is not required. It is obvious – save lives.

Concept Qualification is down to a quick check of feasibility and risks.

Phase-gate approach is down to a simple success criterion for the next set of steps, along with risk assessment and mitigation.

The key to success is a clear definition of the problem, accessible resources, and constraints. It is generally a very short duration project with serious resource limitations. Ideas and options need to be generated rapidly and evaluated instantly. The leader must leverage all the existing talent and knowledge since there is no time to develop talent or research. While the team is working a prime path, someone ought to be ready with an alternate path in parallel. Communication has got to be at the top priority. Risk must come down quickly. I learned a lot from a former US Navy nurse who was in our cohort at the Rensselaer Polytechnic business program, and a customer who is a former US Army Special Forces.

Example – Apollo-13 Homecoming

One of the most outstanding real-world examples of Crisis Innovation is the Apollo-13 event that turned a near-certain disaster into a spectacular save. A very successful failure. Apollo-13 had taken off from earth on its way to the moon with 3 astronauts onboard. Shortly after takeoff, there was an explosion that severely incapacitated the rocket and put the lives of the astronauts in jeopardy. While the technical issues solved by the Mission Control were many, the most critical one was that the astronauts were running out of oxygen to breathe. Their expired CO_2 was not being removed and they were getting lethargic and hypoxic. They could die before they could return to earth. To solve this issue, engineers had to use the astronauts limited resources (supplies available in the space capsule itself) to adapt equipment so that a 'square filter would fit into a round filter hole' as quickly as possible. It was a matter of life and death, and it required engineering experts in all fields to collaborate and engage. The beauty was the clarity of problem definition, in very simple terms – *"We need to make this... fit into a hole made for this... using only this and nothing else."* It worked, and the astronauts made it safely back to earth.

There were a series of other innovative actions taken during the entire flight that saved the crew. This happened in 1970; however, the methods and principles are just as applicable today. Another remarkable achievement of mission control was quickly developing procedures for powering up the Command Module after its long, cold sleep. Flight controllers wrote the documents for this innovation in a few hours, instead of days.

Of course, in addition to Crisis Innovation, there was outstanding leadership – full of inspiration and convincing belief that success is around the corner.

The recent example is around the coronavirus pandemic. World has seen a vast spectrum of Crisis Innovation from makeshift hospitals, ventilators, hand sanitizers, face masks, rapid testing, social distancing, distance learning, etc. We will cover this topic in the next chapter.

A project running late is usually not a crisis, but often referred to as such. However, if your product is misbehaving with a customer/market, then the media can turn it into a crisis, e.g. Takata airbags or Toyota sticky pedal.

Burst Innovation

Key Characteristics

Objective: Rapid and affordable innovation to enable business turnaround or to combat the sudden emergence of competitive threat in the marketplace. It is not as serious as Crisis Innovation. There are no human lives at stake. Only business financials are challenged.
Purpose: Financial, ~~Technical, Social, Sustainability.~~
Profiles: Agile Follower, ~~Smart Forecaster, Visionary Trendsetter.~~

Key Process Elements

Market is typically a direct competitor or an external uncontrollable situation; with direction coming from the CEO.

Customer insight is just as important as for Evolutionary Innovation or a normal day. But the data may be limited due to available time frames. If this is in response to the call of the CEO, then the direction should contain the required information.

Ideation should be open-ended in terms of options, but constrained by accessible resources, due to the schedule pressure to produce results.

Value Propositions can be multiple, simultaneous, and all over the place in terms of options and follow through. The team will have to deal with limited customer insight and might require multiple iterations between customer insight-ideation-value prop. If possible, you should call representative customers.

Purpose Check is important when ideation is broad and open-ended.

Concept Qualification can be difficult due to a shortage of time in data gathering and verification. Multiple concepts need to be qualified simultaneously. A deep and quick market search is advisable. Be prepared for a few iterations.

Phase-gate approach must be taken very seriously, and gatekeepers must be empowered to push back on schedule pressure. The final review should be done by the leadership team.

The key to success is preparation. Start with identifying the design space using multiple inputs: company growth objectives, new market development, the state of the technology, competitive landscape, and the important projects that could benefit from new technology. Then select the right working group. It's best to keep the group small yet diverse, with several important business functions represented. To change the thinking, the event should be held at a location different than where the day-to-day work is done – at an off-site location. Provide good food to help the working group feel the event is a bit special. Happy hour can do magic with the ideation the next day when the team feels bonded.

All this should be communicated and documented in a charter. This charter has specific boundaries to keep the team focused. Money is generally not an issue. How much can you spend anyway in a few days on a few people? Access to the right participants within the company should not be an issue. An external facilitator is a must.

It is emotionally challenging to do work that destroys your business model and obsoletes your best products, but that is how it is with innovation. But for motivation, think about this – if your business model is going away, it is best if you make it go away, rather than your competition. But if your competition does end up changing the game and taking your business, I know how they will do it – Burst Innovation.

Example – Burst out of the Pandemic Bubble

We are right now going through a pandemic. It is so relevant and timely, that I have decided to add a full chapter on this topic, which further elaborates on the process.

Bold Innovation

Key Characteristics

Objective: Large scale, complex, high budget, multi-year, unique system of products and services. For many people, it could be a dream project before it is all done, and a sight-seeing or a story after it is done.
Purpose: Financial, Technical, Social, Sustainability.
Profiles: ~~Agile Follower~~, ~~Smart Forecaster~~, Visionary Trendsetter.

Key Process Elements

Market can be specific, niche, or mass, single sector or multi-segmented, even an ecosystem.
Customer insight can be very difficult, because there may be no data. Focus groups, interviews would likely have a poor outcome. Purpose and values are more important in this case.

Ideation will be hierarchical starting from system and rolling down to products and technologies. It may roll back up and iterate across various domains and disciplines, due to complexity. A Bold Innovation project will require innovation in almost every discipline from design, technologies, portfolio, manufacturing, construction, integration, sales, financing, pricing, life cycle maintenance, branding, business models, and so on.

Value Propositions will be in large numbers, again hierarchical or nested, requiring a series of reviews and cross-checks.

Purpose Check on the whole system is a must before the venture launch.

Concept Qualification can be difficult due to hierarchical nature limiting the capability to estimate returns at the elemental level. The good part is that the system acts as a single big portfolio, where some pieces will make a lot of sense whereas the cost will just have to be eaten up for some; while the system as a whole makes sense in the end. The risks and uncertainties must be quantified and addressed throughout.

Creating the full set of nested Concept Qualifications (detailed plan or proposal) is a project in itself. It is a good idea to validate individual concepts and verify the integration.

Ethics Check is important in such large system innovations.

Phase-gate approach must be taken very seriously and gates need to be nested to address the hierarchy. This nesting also creates a schedule pressure on all of the elements of the system. The project will probably be significantly ahead of its time and might lead to many new technologies with diverse applications as byproducts. Such items ought to be captured at the phase-gates.

The key to success is clarity of purpose. This may be an iconic symbol or mission for humanity or something in between. Define and communicate the vision and purpose. Ensure connectivity of all projects, but allow them to innovate and pivot individually, within boundaries. Employee morale is very important in creating Bold Innovation, they must believe that such a project is feasible and worth sacrificing.

Example – Taming the Himalayan Rivers

Two major rivers, Beas and Sutlej, flow out of the Himalayas and reach a point where they are separated by a crow fly distance of ~24 miles and have an elevation difference of approximately 1099 ft. The waters of Beas are continuous flow from ice-melt. This realization offered an opportunity to divert Beas and drop it into Sutlej for hydropower with estimated potential for 1,000 MW.

The civil construction plan approved in 1963 included two tunnels ~8 miles long and 25-28 feet in diameter through the hills, with a 7-mile hydel channel through the valley in between. The project was commissioned in 1977, with a payback period of about a few years. Today, it pays for itself almost every month.

The most advanced calculating machine was the slide rule. All navigation inside the tunnel was through a line of sight survey device called a theodolite. The risk levels were so high, that I do not wish to write them in here.

I grew up on this project, visiting every month during 1972-77 as a middle school student with my father. My dad used to tell me stories of problems and creative solutions every day. That is the nature of a bold vision project. I have been into the tunnel several times in the train, jeep, on foot, and even had a chance to cross through the entire tunnel just weeks before it was all filled with water forever. During that time, I would come back home and build working models of earthmoving machines with pieces of Meccano. Perhaps, that is where the spirit of innovation all started.

Example – The Big Boiler

BrightSource Energy and General Electric (GE) have built a 121 MW Ashalim Solar Thermal Power Station in Israel's Negev desert. More than 50,000 computer-controlled mirrors track the sun on two axes and reflect sunlight onto a steel boiler on top of a 250-meter tower. Electricity production commenced in September 2019.

I had a good fortune of leading a fine team of engineers to design the solar boiler, as my last corporate job at Alstom Power, before it was acquired by GE. At the outset, it appeared to be very simple; just flip the traditional boiler inside-out as if it is a shirt. Instead of burning coal inside, we capture the heat from outside. And everything 'balance of plant' which is traditionally outside, now gets packaged inside.

As the saying goes *'the devil is in the detail!'* We had so many unanswered questions, and new ones coming up in every weekly meeting.

- Do we have enough space inside? No! What can we do?
- How will we raise a few million pounds of steel, 250m up in the air?
- How do we prepare for the unknown?
- How do we know who to hire for R&D?
- How do we assess the technical risks of a thing that large, hot, and high?
- What is the right material, given the temperature uncertainty?
- How do we maintain coating integrity, up there, exposed?
- Where are the federal compliance requirements?

In addition to boiler design that was our responsibility, we used to have fun discussing other technical challenges.

- How do we assure focus of reflected beam from long distance?
- How do we keep these mirrors clean all the time?
- How do we install 100s of mirrors every day in a desert with no roads?
- How do we assure safety during construction and operation?

I attribute the design success to incredible teamwork; the diverse team we built over 90 days, with ~40% non-boiler discipline experts. We prepared the team to always ask – what else do we not know?

We would isolate what is known and what is new, we will breakdown the new into pieces, until we can answer questions at an elemental level and then roll them back up to integrated solutions. We used to have brainstorming sessions and risk mitigation meetings every week on diverse technical topics, and then run the ideas through an experience-based check. Our modus operandi was to record/address every concern and be ready for unaware – unknown. Throughout the design process, we were clear on priorities: safety, system performance, and cost. It was a good run. I learned a lot about renewable energy, boilers, team dynamics, and Bold Innovation.

Some other examples of Bold Innovation include – Designer babies, Human mission to Mars, Floating city, Hyperloop transportation.

I wish I had the tools that I now talk about in this book series, during my time leading the big boiler. Perhaps desire to share that experience and solutions to everyday leadership needs is what led to creating this work.

Frugal Innovation

Key Characteristics

Objective: Overcoming harsh constraints by improvising an effective solution using limited resources[46]. Crisis Innovation is usually full of Frugal Innovations on the go. Reverse is generally not true.

Purpose: ~~Financial~~, ~~Technical~~, Social, ~~Sustainability.~~

Profiles: Agile Follower, Smart Forecaster, Visionary Trendsetter.

Key Process Elements

Market is typically marginal, under-served customers, or personal.

Customer insight is a visible problem close to the heart of the innovator.

Ideation is all about 'work with what you've got.' Often, it is a spark of an idea that matches the problem insight.

Value Proposition is generally simple, a small effort using scarce financial and natural resources to provide a high-value solution to a specific concern.

Purpose Check is helpful, but typically not required.

---

[46] Jugaad - A New Growth Formula for Corporate America; N Radjou, J Prabhu, S Ahuja; Book 2010.

Concept Qualification is not about seeking sophistication or perfection by over-engineering products, but rather about developing a 'good enough' solution that gets the job done.

Phase-gate is generally missing.

Example – SELCO's Affordable Energy

Harish Hande, founded SELCO in Bangalore, India in 1995. By 2010, while the Indian government was still deliberating on how to effectively deliver electricity to the 600 million Indians who live off the grid, Harish had already sold more than 100,000 modular solar lighting systems in the remotest regions of India. His firm SELCO employed an innovative business model that relied on a cost-effective grassroots distribution network to deliver affordable electricity on a pay-as-you-go basis to underserved Indian shops, households, and schools in order to power their everyday socio-economic activities. SELCO's frugal just-in-time energy distribution system — as opposed to the always-on but wasteful electricity grid — brought more value to more Indians at less cost, and it is both environmentally and economically sustainable. SELCO's business model is an outcome of the frugal mindset.

SELCO[47] is also a good example of Purposeful Innovation, or a purpose-driven company, *"Delivering Last-Mile Sustainable Energy Solutions that Improve Quality of Life and Socio-economic Development for the Poor."*

Kanak Das, who lives in a remote village in North East India got tired of riding his bicycle on roads full of potholes and bumps. Rather than complaining, he turned it to his advantage by retrofitting his bicycle with a device that will convert the shocks it receives into potential energy, allowing him to use the stored energy to ride his bicycle faster and with less physical effort.

---

[47] http://www.selco-india.com/

Open Innovation

Key Characteristics

Objectives: Better products, services, and solutions, using external ideas as well as internal ideas, and internal and external paths to market. Other objectives may include speed to market, talent, and knowledge augmentation, developing platform-based businesses, becoming competitively unpredictable, risk mitigation, cost reduction, to address stubborn challenges, getting feedback on early prototypes, allowing consumers to contribute to the design, creating internal motivation/unrest, changing the corporate culture, …

Purpose: Financial, Technical, Social, Sustainability.

Profiles: ~~Agile Follower~~, Smart Forecaster, Visionary Trendsetter.

> *According to ISO,* **open innovation** *is defined as 'process for the management of information and knowledge sharing and flows across the boundaries of the organization with regard to innovation.' Open innovation can be a collaborative process involving several parties, or even facilitated by the presence of an innovation ecosystem or value network. (ISO56000:2020 Clause 3.6.5)*

Key Process Elements

Market can be anything.

Customer insight can come from external partners as well.

Legal check is important before going out of the company to protect intellectual property, or from commerce control or national security angle when operating internationally.

Ideation from outside the team responsible for the project is what led to the term Open Innovation. You can go as far out as you like, constrained only legally and ethically. It could be in the form of a solicitation over the web, on well-defined problems, or even open-ended areas of interest.

Value Proposition may or may not be developed jointly with external idea sources.

Purpose Check helps to find and align partners.

Concept Qualification should typically be done internally and may offer a bit of a challenge, because the value proposition is coming from outside and the idea originator may not be accessible for iterative improvement.

Ethics Check is important before accepting an external idea.

Phase-gate approach could benefit from the participation of idea originators.

Example – Lego Opens New Doors

Lego activates its users through its Create and Share site as well as the Lego Ideas site. The 'Create and Share' site lets Lego community members share their designs and Lego pictures, while the 'Ideas' site aims for new product releases.

As an example, the mini-Big Bang Theory Lego set is a community-based product that originated in the Lego Ideas. When the number of supporters reaches 10k, Lego evaluates the design and the design can hit the stores under the Lego Ideas product label. The idea for mini-Big Bang Theory was submitted over 2 years ago and it took the project over 10 months to get from the Ideas site to production. When the product ideas are approved for production, the original community members that ideated the product also get monetary compensation.

The community provides Lego with thousands of new ideas annually, which means that Lego has a steady flow of free ideas that people are already waiting to buy. This Open Innovation approach in their product design phase is said to be one of the core factors for Lego's successful brand. It has been one of the things that saved their brand and made them stay at the top of the market.

It is also a good example of early customer engagement, or user shared vision. When the users interact with one another and tell you what they would want to see on the store shelves, you probably have ready demand, and can save a lot of resources on market research and reduce the inherent risk in R&D.

Classified Innovation

Key Characteristics

Objective: Creating new technologies, products, services, business models, relationships with utmost secrecy.

Purpose: ~~Financial,~~ Technical, ~~Social,~~ ~~Sustainability.~~

Profiles: ~~Agile Follower~~, Smart Forecaster, Visionary Trendsetter.

Key Process Elements

Market typically national defense sector or corporate leadership.

Customer insight is usually a very clear direction with limited information, making details difficult and uncertain to come by.

Ideation is typically open-ended in scope, with closed-door limited participation.

Value Proposition is likely to be strong and clear.

Purpose Check is almost a pre-requisite.

Concept Qualification is likely to have significant uncertainty on one hand, and little financial constraints on the other hand.

Ethics Check is important.

Phase-gate approach needs significant rigor in the process to assure risk reduction, typically high in the beginning.

Example – Shh...

I have never worked on a Classified Innovation project to provide a good example. I guess, if you get called into work on one, you can apply the tools from this book, staying within compliance of information handling.

Breakthrough Innovation

Key Characteristics

Objective: Specific significant technological advance that makes a large impact on the efficiency or cost of a given product, service, or a process; leading to significant market share capture.
Purpose: ~~Financial~~, Technical, Social, ~~Sustainability.~~
Profiles: ~~Agile Follower~~, ~~Smart Forecaster~~, Visionary Trendsetter.

Key Process Elements

Market typically materials, technology products, and consumer goods.
Customer insight is somewhat clear from the deep analysis of desires.
Ideation is typically open-ended around step change.
Value Proposition is likely to be strong and clear.
Purpose Check is almost a pre-requisite.
Concept Qualification is likely to have significant uncertainty on one hand, and significant financial constraints on the other hand. These are typically a combination of many innovations to tackle a specific challenge or opportunity, and may require multiple concept qualifications, even nested.
Ethics Check is important.
Phase-gate approach needs significant rigor in the process to assure risk reduction.

Example – Elon Musk Breaks Through the Established Barriers

Tesla has been cited all over from incremental to disruptive, depending upon the eye of the beholder. I am inclined to agree with Jesse Nieminen[48], that the core technologies of Tesla's vehicles, both electric motors and lithium-ion batteries have been around for quite some time, which Tesla

---

[48] Breakthrough Innovation – What Are They, and How Do You Create One?' Jesse Nieminen, https://www.viima.com/blog/breakthrough-innovation Jan 03; 2020.

refined in somewhat incremental nature. However, the way they have put together these innovations and are constantly and rapidly kept improving them; such that they've been able to challenge and surpass internal combustion engine cars in many ways; is certainly radical. The advances in self-driving technology would qualify to be disruptive.

A visually stunning innovation in the space sector has been the ability to land and reuse rockets that have been to orbit, to dramatically decrease the costs of space launches. While reusable rockets are quite widely considered to be a Breakthrough Innovation, it is a combination of quite a few new technologies and systems.

Neuralink founded by Elon Musk in 2016 is developing implantable brain-machine interfaces. The company hired several high-profile neuroscientists from various universities and a staff of almost 100 to work on a *'sewing machine-like'* device capable of implanting very thin (4 to 6 µm in width) threads into the brain. So far, they have demonstrated a system that reads information from a lab rat via 1,500 electrodes and they are anticipated to start experiments with humans in 2020.

These technological breakthroughs can cause market disruption.

Disruptive Innovation

Key Characteristics

Objective: Rapid capture of market share with completely new norms.
Purpose: Financial, Technical, ~~Social, Sustainability.~~
Profiles: ~~Agile Follower, Smart Forecaster~~, Visionary Trendsetter.

Key Process Elements

Market could be any, ranging from niche (space) to mass (uber) market
Customer insight is a usually a very clear white space or beachhead.
Ideation is the key element of disruption.
Value Proposition is likely to be very simple, and contagious.

Purpose Check is almost a pre-requisite.

Concept Qualification is very difficult due to significant uncertainty.

Ethics Check is important. It could be very difficult to think through where some technology disruptions can go.

Phase-gate approach needs significant rigor and might lead to significant rework. The team ought to be open to turnbacks.

Example – Netflix'it or get Blockbusted!

In 2000, Reed Hastings, Netflix founder proposed a partnership with Blockbuster's CEO John Antioco and his team in a meeting. The idea was that Netflix would run Blockbuster's brand online and Antioco's firm would promote Netflix in its stores. The Netflix founder Hastings got laughed out of the room. Blockbuster declined to purchase Netflix at $50M. In 2010, Blockbuster went bankrupt and Netflix is at $246B company today (2020).

Blockbuster's CEO, Antioco, was considered a retail genius with a long history of successes. Blockbuster's business model had a weakness that wasn't clear at the time. The ugly truth—and the company's Achilles heel— was that the company's profits were highly dependent on penalizing its patrons. At the same time, Netflix had certain distinct advantages. By eschewing retail locations, it lowered costs and could afford to offer its customers a far greater variety. Instead of charging to rent videos, it offered subscriptions, which made annoying late fees unnecessary. Customers could watch a video for as long as they wanted or return it and get a new one.

Netflix proved to be a very disruptive business model innovation, despite being a small, niche service at the time, it had the potential to upend Blockbuster's well-oiled machine. While Netflix's model had some compelling aspects, it also had some obvious disadvantages. Without retail locations, it was hard for people to find it. Moreover, because its customers received their videos by mail, the service was somewhat cumbersome. People couldn't just pick up a movie for the night on their way home.

Netflix mindset to innovate brought them early into the streaming service in 2007. Netflix had had its own issues with the changes in technology, branding, and pricing and split its DVD by mail and online streaming services into two different companies, each focusing on one business model. Amid strong customer backlash, Netflix quickly changed its business model back to the Netflix brand – though they continued to split the pricing model between the online streaming and DVD by mail. By 2016, it joined the list of Top 10 innovative companies - *Apple, Google, Tesla, Microsoft, Amazon, Netflix (biz models), Samsung, Toyota, Facebook, and IBM.*

More on Disruptive Innovation

Some of the other visible and notable disruptions include, Amazon for retail and now even product search; WhatsApp and WeChat for messaging and now even supporting collaborative business engagement, Tesla for the auto industry, Uber in mobility, and more. Amazon could be coming to other industries as well.

Disruptive Innovations cause ripple effects in other industries. The smartphone has killed so many other products – magnifier, camera, calculator, calendar, notepad, alarm clock, music player, wallet, games, GPS, flashlight, compass, light meter, gaussmeter, sound meter, TV remote, and the list is growing. We already talked about driverless cars that will hurt many other sectors such as parking lots, highways, Dept of Motor Vehicles, auto insurance, highway patrol, emergency rooms, injury lawyers.

As an innovator or strategic planner, be cognizant about how your business may get disrupted by a disruption in the same or a completely different sector, or by a business such as Amazon. A new 'Death by Amazon' index was released in 2019 by the investment research firm CFRA (Center for Financial Research and Analysis). This tracks the stocks its analysts believe could be short-seller targets given their vulnerabilities to competition from Amazon. The index is full of home goods and electronics retailers like Party City and Bed Bath & Beyond, some of which have seen their entire market value wiped out in recent years.

Business Model Innovation

Key Characteristics

Objective: New revenue sources by improving value perception and customer engagement. Think of these three types in creating value (efficiency, effectiveness).

Servicize: when the product is delivered as a service.

Uberize: change the way buyers and sellers connect.

Amazonize: restructure the delivery channel or eliminate steps.

Purpose: Financial, ~~Technical~~, ~~Social~~, ~~Sustainability~~.

Profiles: ~~Agile Follower~~, Smart Forecaster, Visionary Trendsetter.

Key Process Elements

Market remains the same, unless the model opens up a whole new segment.

Customer insight is somewhat clear, with an easy opportunity to field test.

Ideation is best when done in an open setting.

Value Proposition is likely to be very simple.

Purpose Check is not required while serving with the same product/service offering.

Concept Qualification is difficult due to uncertainty and intangible benefits.

Ethics Check is important, when changing how value is perceived and cash flows.

Phase-gate approach is important and deserves attention.

Example – Netflix Again

The Netflix example above is a great one for the business model as well.

Back in 2017, while working with a client in India, where we started implementing this innovation framework, I got into a partnership arrangement where in exchange for my coaching services, their IT team would help us convert the methodology into a cloud-based SaaS platform. The outcome is EinFrame, available in the market for use.

Digital Disruption of Business Model: It is the application of digital technologies to a company's operations and customer interactions to improve operational efficiency and create better customer experience.

Process Innovation

Key Characteristics

Objective: Efficiency and effectiveness in accomplishing the same output, such as reduce cost, accelerate activity, improve safety, reduce footprint, and any other value enhancement to design, manufacturing, delivery, and maintenance activity.

Purpose: Financial, ~~Technical, Social, Sustainability.~~

Profiles: Agile Follower, Smart Forecaster, ~~Visionary Trendsetter~~.

Key Process Elements

Market typically is the owner of the process, or the business unit head.

Customer insight is clear, very often quantifiable.

Ideation is generally an employee originated, internally discussed, or facilitated through an external process consultant. Many new opportunities have emerged with the advent of Industry 4.0 that require awareness.

Value Proposition is likely to be very simple.

Purpose Check is not required while serving with the same product/service offering.

Concept Qualification is very easy with traditional solutions, but somewhat difficult with industry 4.0 technologies due to lack of experience with implementation, acceptance, and training.

Ethics Check is important, when changing how value is created.

Phase-gate approach is simple but deserves attention to ensure objectivity and independence in implementation and remove any bias or conflict of interest.

Examples – All Over

This is the second most common form of innovation, next to Evolutionary products. Most companies are doing it all the time. The entire subject of lean and six-sigma has been driving this for decades now.

Caution: Managers with funds to invest in innovation gravitate towards this form, to show near-term progress, and visible tangible financial benefits. Senior managers tend to like such managers and promote them for performance. Good leaders ought to strike a balance between process and product innovations.

Workbench Innovation

Key Characteristics

Objective: Personal gains in terms of time savings or comfort, common with an employee in an organization, quite often graduating to the level of process innovation if and when broadly accepted.
Purpose: Personal, Financial, ~~Technical~~, ~~Social~~, ~~Sustainability~~.
Profiles: Agile Follower, ~~Smart Forecaster~~, ~~Visionary Trendsetter~~.

Key Process Elements

Market is oneself, or the supervisor at the most.
Customer insight is very clear. You know yourself and accept who you are.
Ideation is typically oneself or maybe a discussion with a close associate.
Value Proposition is trivial.
Purpose Check is not required.
Concept Qualification is not applicable. Typically, it is a trial and error or adapt.
Ethics Check is very important; driven by a personal moral compass. Creative activity for personal financial gains, or to skimp on compliance, safety, or quality, is cheating. It may still be innovative but unethical.
Phase-gate approach is important and deserves attention.

Examples – All Over

Every day, all of us, are looking for ways to do our job a little better than yesterday, whether it is at home or office. It could be as simple as changing a recessed light bulb on a 20 feet ceiling, fixing a broken tool on the CNC machine, arranging groceries on the store shelf, optimizing a delivery route, and so on.

Responsible Innovation

Key Characteristics

Objective: Innovation for social good, humanity, or a sustainable planet.
Purpose: ~~Financial~~, ~~Technical~~, Social, Sustainability.
Profiles: ~~Agile Follower~~, Smart Forecaster, Visionary Trendsetter.

Key Process Elements

Market is from regional community to all of humanity.
Customer insight is somewhat clear, with limited data, mixed with emotions.
Ideation is best when done in an open setting.
Value Proposition is likely to be very simple, and contagious.
Purpose Check is almost a pre-requisite.
Concept Qualification is difficult due to uncertainty and intangible benefits.
Ethics Check is important.
Phase-gate approach is important and deserves attention.

Examples – Renew, Repurpose, Recycle, ... wherever possible

The entire field of renewable energy, with a specific objective of reducing carbon footprint classifies to be a Responsible Innovation.

Biodegradable plastics have been developed that can be decomposed by the action of living organisms, usually microbes, into water, carbon dioxide, and biomass. These are commonly produced with renewable raw materials, micro-organisms, petrochemicals, or combinations of all three.

The company Ocean Cleanup[49] founded by a 25-year old Boyan Slat has developed the first scalable solution to efficiently intercept plastic in rivers before it reaches the oceans. By placing Interceptors in 1000 strategic locations in rivers around the world, they aim to halt 80% of plastic from entering the oceans in five years. Their passive cleanup method uses the natural oceanic forces to rapidly and cost-effectively clean up the plastic already in the oceans. With a full fleet of cleanup systems in the Great Pacific Garbage Patch, they aim to clean up 50% of its plastic every five years. After several ups and downs, in October 2019, they announced that the system is capturing and collecting plastic debris, from massive ghost nets down to microplastics one millimeter in size. The Ocean Cleanup has also planned to create a value chain based on their collected debris, with the aim of funding continued cleanup operations. At the end of 2019, they announced the intention to develop attractive, sustainable products made from material collected in the Great Pacific Garbage Patch, and bring it to market by Sept 2020. The interesting part of such stories is funding. They are offering the opportunity to get onboard through a 50 EUR/USD donation to get first access to the first product ever made from the plastic recovered from the Great Pacific Garbage Patch. Where are all the plastic manufacturers? Should they feel responsible for cleanup as well? Do we need a system akin to carbon-credits so that the market forces can take care of the imbalance?

Open-source or Crowd-source Innovation

I am not sure what to call it. It is something we have seen before, many times, but never formally defined it, or perhaps it can't be defined.

---

[49] The Largest Cleanup in History; https://theoceancleanup.com/

Key Characteristics

Objective: Crisis Innovation for humanity, with no business model. A large number of people engage in some form or the other, use materials, machines, and products easily available, create a prototype or a few pieces, and let everyone freely copy/download the design for mass production near the point of use.

Purpose: ~~Financial~~, ~~Technical~~, Social, ~~Sustainability~~.

Profiles: Agile Follower, ~~Smart Forecaster~~, Visionary Trendsetter.

Key Process Elements

Market is the humans, or their caretakers whose lives are in jeopardy.

Customer insight is about rapid & continuous situational awareness and assessment.

Ideation is the key component, needs to be rapid, exhaustive, but constrained by accessible resources (people, tools, materials, energy, mobility, devices, MedTech)

Value Proposition is clear, and requires no discussion, the outcome is to be distributed freely.

Purpose Check is not required. It is obvious.

Concept Qualification is down to a quick check of feasibility and risks.

Phase-gate approach is down to a simple success criterion for the next set of steps, along with risk assessment and mitigation.

Example – Creativity during the Coronavirus Pandemic

Three items were in real short supply – face masks, hand sanitizer, and ventilators. The first few months of Q1 in 2020 saw so many global efforts in addressing this demand.

Dyson, a vacuum cleaner company, designed and built an entirely new ventilator, called the 'CoVent,' in less than 10 days. They will make 15,000 and donate 5,000. In the USA, Ford, 3M, GE, GM, and Tesla pledged to make ventilators. Local incubators assembled ventilators.

This time also saw an emergence of **'Open-source Ventilator'**, which is defined as "A disaster-situation ventilator made using a freely-licensed design, and ideally, freely-available components and parts. Designs, components, and parts may be anywhere from completely reverse-engineered to completely new creations, components may be adaptations of various inexpensive existing products, and special hard-to-find and/or expensive parts may be 3-D-printed instead of sourced. A new design configuration was created in 3 days of a Hackaday project; and on March 20, 2020 Irish Health Services began reviewing designs. A prototype was designed and tested in Colombia as well. The Polish company *Urbicum* reports successful testing of a 3D-printed open-source prototype device called *VentilAid* using compressed air. The makers describe it as a last resort device when professional equipment is missing. The design was publicly available.

3D printing community has gotten on top of face masks, after seeing the N95 shortage gripping the healthcare workers, while many of the big players are struggling and faltering. Maker space down my street is printing masks. A team of high school students with a FabLab in Charlotte, led by two Doctor parents have an ongoing GoFundMe: *'Save Lives with 3D Printed Face Shields'* is impressive and inspiring. Families at home, are stitching face masks. Indian Institute of Technology (Ropar) has created a frugal solution: wax-dipped handkerchief to act as a face mask. There are probably 100s of more stories all over and helping locally. It is an era where small agile players are stepping up to meet the demands of humanity.

HP Inc. and partners mobilized to create 3D printed face mask and face shield solutions. They have offered more than 1,000 3D printed parts already delivered to local hospitals close to their 3D R&D centers around the world. They have made their and other company's 3D models free to download for local production.

Breweries started making hand sanitizers. From Pernod to BrewDog, companies are using their alcohol expertise to help fight the coronavirus. Melissa Hanesworth and Tara Engel at the New York-based North American division of Pernod Ricard retooled the corporation's distilleries for industrial quantities of hand gel. It was a bat-out-of-hell turnaround. Within days, the facility in Fort Smith, Ark., where it makes Malibu coconut rum and Seagram's gin, had produced 1,000 gallons of hand sanitizer. By the next day, the US President was lauding the company at a news conference as a shining example of corporations stepping up to the challenge of fighting the global pandemic. The regional head, Ann Mukherjee says, "a time of crisis is not what builds your character, it's what reveals it."

These stories touched my heart once again. I have seen these in movies, heard from my grandfather, who was in the British Army in WWII, and my dad during India-Pakistan separation. Schools getting shut down and working from home is a rather easy part of the equation.

Dark Innovation

This is exactly the opposite of Open-source Innovation.

Key Characteristics

Objective: Intentional destruction of property, life, or social stability.

I do not wish to discuss this.

Example – 9.11

The terrorist attack of 9/11/2001 in the USA is an example of Dark Innovation.

Let's Summarize

There is no single unique process for innovation that works for every situation. The idea-problem matchmaking activity varies depending upon the availability of resources and time. The best-case scenario is when a purpose-driven company can generate many great ideas for a clearly defined problem.

Let's Take a Selfie

 # My favorite case for each of type, that I have been involved in.

Workbench   ___

Process   ___

Evolutionary   ___

Peripheral   ___

Eco-adaptive   ___

Crisis   ___

Burst   ___

Bold   ___

Frugal   ___

Open   ___

Classified   ___

Breakthrough   ___

Disruptive   ___

Responsible   ___

Business Model ___

Open Source   ___

7.   *Value Chain in a Tough Time*

TOUGH TIMES NEVER LAST, BUT TOUGH PEOPLE DO
– ROBERT H SCHULLER

One day early morning in January 2020, on way to a client site, it occurred to me that China shutdown from Coronavirus will cause a serious supply chain disruption to this client. This was before the US had the first confirmed case, and we had not anticipated the impending closedown. Thinking ahead, I realized that I must find a way to help my clients before it is too late. And then, the possibility that all of my customers could be impacted jolted me. Which means, my practice could either sink or soar depending upon how I prepared to help my client base, and how I pivoted my services, when the world changed on me.

At the client site, I opened the meeting with, *"I think we should pivot from Strategic Planning to Strategic Readiness or Strategic Preparedness."* The team felt that I was overthinking. Why would we suddenly change the scope of our 5-year Strategy Plan exercise, when we were just about to wrap it up.

I started calling my friends in China and the ISO team around the world to understand the situation. It took me a few days to fully grasp the magnitude of likely scenarios that may emerge. There were not many reports or predictions for the US in Late January. US media was still focused on democratic primary election debates, and the DC administration was playing a low key in the election year.

I reviewed my strengths and weaknesses in the context of likely market trends and scenarios. I went into an ideation burst with my partners Vaibhav and Prashant, and identified a couple of new products/services that could help businesses deal with the pandemic. Then I quickly developed a **Burst Innovation Workshop for Coronavirus.** By this time, McKenzie, Boston

Consulting, Gartner, and other consultants had all started coming out with recommendations, primarily to survive the crisis. By mid-March 2020, the media was 90% occupied by the pandemic and the entire world was praying for humanity. The nation went into shutdown, and I stayed home to finish these books.

The CDC, the World Health Organization (WHO), the White House, and the State Governors regularly guided the public and businesses through the crisis. Everyone was looking forward to coming out of this, to rebuild the economy in a whole new world. A world with new norms. A world where many industries would have seen a 10-year equivalent change, virtually overnight. The phrase *'It happened in a blink of an eye'*, became a first-hand experience.

All of us found ourselves *"Out of the Box,"* kicked out by the Coronavirus. We entered an *'Era of the Innovator'.* A time-period where we will need **Burst Innovation Events,** lots of them, all over the world. That call inspired me to add this chapter which is anchored in the realities of Coronavirus, but applicable to any human or business crisis.

Burst Innovation Event

A **Burst Innovation Event** is a short, sudden, and intense innovation effort to quickly resolve a challenging business or humanitarian situation. It is characterized by a clearly defined near-term objective and speed of execution. The steps can be graphically depicted as follows.

Your Next Step in Crisis

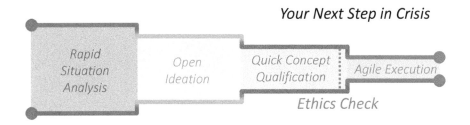

Market insight is replaced with situation analysis and scenario planning. Ideation goes wide open but bounded to scenarios. Concept qualification has less of market analysis and more assumptions around uncertainty, and execution needs additional agility. Let's look at each of these steps.

Rapid Situation Analysis

Preliminary Objective

Start with whatever little understanding you have for the situation in hand. List what you know for sure, and what you have heard so far, yet to be verified, and draft a preliminary objective. Depending upon the leadership frame of mind, it could be a *recovery* type objective such as restore supply chain, find alternate customers, or prepare for an exit. Or it could even be a *growth* type objective such as scout for businesses up for sale, hire talent that is suddenly available, redefine product portfolio, etc. It can even be a combination *recover-and-grow*. Keep it simple until you have a better situation analysis.

External and Internal Context

Now define the context in three categories and separate what is known for sure and what may be a speculation, or fear factor, yet to be verified. You may choose to take quick actions to verify them or leave them as assumptions to carry through into the next step.

- **Broad External Context (no direct business connection)** This is what is happening to you, completely out of your control, and is happening at scales that you must adapt and respond to. PESTEL falls into this category.
- **Close External Context (direct business connection)** This is related to your immediate environment – customers, suppliers, community, region, essentially items partially out of your control and are happening at scales that are comparable to your business; or in your vicinity. You may have to accept/ignore/negotiate around them. One possible

challenge can be when your customer/supplier is also in the same crisis, and you cannot anticipate their moves.

- **Internal Context (your own business)** This is related to your business – employees, capabilities, funding reserves, inventories, contracts, … essentially items mostly (if not all) under your control and are happening at scales that are within your means to manage, handle, or leverage as needed.

Conduct a quick and narrow SWOT analysis of your current business situation and the uncertain delivery value stream, in the context identified above. It may or may not be a crisis. It may even be an unprecedented opportunity. Some of visionaries will be excited, about what will unfold in the coming years.

Summarize all of this for presentation to the executives, so they can revise or replace the preliminary objective with a quantified charter and allocate resources. Separate the bad news (pains, fears, and losses), the good news (gains, wins, neutral) and the unknowns (yet to unfold or assess).

Scenarios and Likely Impact

Now define three scenarios (optimistic, realistic, and pessimistic) and predict the impact (near-term and long-term) for each of these scenarios on your purpose. State what the success should look like in the near-term and far term. Think through the ripple effects across industries and society.

Clear Leadership Charter

Based on the situation analysis and the scenarios, it is time to define *"What would success look like?"* This is the real executive decision, and often not an easy one. What is the realistic target, the minimum acceptable, and the stretch goal? Also, you may have to look at it from multiple perspectives, such as customers, employees, owners, society, just like a balanced scorecard. Although all perspectives may not be important. It is good to ask that question.

Write down the actual charter with quantified and time-bound objectives; Resources and sources; limitations and constraints; and whatever else is important. Near-term and long-term objectives should be defined separately. Long-term objectives will have to be reviewed after the near-term performance. It is OK to be exact, however, my preferred position is to provide a bit of a range to allow for creativity and uncertainty.

Open Ideation

All of the Chapter-3 on Structured Ideation is applicable here. Just start with the leadership charter as strategic objective and work through a set of tactical objectives. It will be good to find ideas that serve multiple sub-objectives. In most cases one would require a portfolio to address the charter.

Make sure to include those crazy thinkers in your organization, because they love to play in an uncertain reality with unacceptable thoughts.

Gut-based Pre-Screening of Ideas and a Theme

I do not like the gut-based idea screening under normal circumstances, because the best ones will be eliminated. But in a crisis, we may not have time to do justice to all ideas. So, pick the top few promising ones and some others as having potential. Affinity based clustering under themes is a possible way to incorporate many of these.

Quick Concept Qualification

Simplified Qualification Canvas

The process in Chapter-4 can be somewhat overwhelming when you are short on time. This can be accelerated with a relatively simpler set of questions, in the **'Crisis Canvas'** below, for each of the promising ideas from the previous step.

Crisis Canvas	
Value Proposition or Idea	
1. Pains / Loss	3. Pain killer
2. Fears	4. Fear buster
Quick Concept Qualification	
5. Risks	6. Risk mitigator
7. Activities	10. Timeline / Cost
8. Resources required	11. Sources for the required resources
9. Skills required	12. Accessible talent

These boxes can be filled in the sequence as numbered.

Start with the concept, idea, or the value proposition in the top box.

1. Pains / Loss from situation analysis.
2. Fears from situation analysis.
3. Pain killer from the proposed concept.
4. Fear buster from the proposed concept.
5. Risk/challenges and any collateral damage from the execution.
6. Risk mitigation actions.
7. Activities to completely execute the idea.
8. Resources required – people, funds, equipment, mobility.
9. Skills required to execute the activities.
10. Associated costs and timeline.
11. Sources for all of the resources listed in 8.
12. Specific individuals that must be called upon to pull it through.

Finalizing the canvas might require some back and forth iteration of the concept, until all items in the right column are acceptable. Notice that each box in the right column is directly dependent upon the box on the left. And each box in the left column is dependent upon the boxes above it.

Quick Validation through Mock Court Room

This is an exercise in validation to bring out any hidden opinions or avoid falling into groupthink. We use the debate form with the deliberate assignment of the devil's role. Split the team into two, add a couple of extra folks to each team who were not a part of it earlier. Let us call them the Oak and Maple teams.

Debate Round 1: Maple team prosecutes the concept, while Oak defends it. Maple is tasked to vehemently oppose the concept, show why it won't work or how it can fail, and challenge everything. Oak is asked to passionately support the concept, how it will work, and show value or answers to Maple's objections.

Debate Round 2: Oak team prosecutes the concept, while Maple defends.

This gives everyone to speak up against any idea without looking like a non-believer. Sometimes it helps to have a couple of *'jury'* folks to see what none of the debaters could see. Executives may sit in and help prioritize improvement actions.

Simple Prioritization

Pick all of the qualified concepts (crisis canvas) and assign a 'likelihood of success' and 'impact when successful' in some relative form – say Low, Med, High. Now use the traditional impact-likelihood matrix to prioritize. Since the analysis has been rather rapid and ad-hoc with assumptions to be verified, some amount of adjustment to priorities based on gut and experience is acceptable. The results of qualified concepts can be summarized for executive approval as (a) prime path, (b) backup paths and triggers, and (c) what not to do.

Review and Approval

At this point executives need to come in and approve the primary path and at least one backup path. This could also be a portfolio of activities and not just a single item. Ensure that approved concepts do not distract you from your primary purpose and are still ethical no matter how tough the times are. This is also a chance to be human; show compassion towards customers, suppliers, employees; by relaxing penalties, flexing schedules, accommodating deliveries, helping with the small stuff, and so on. Be particularly cognizant of any vulnerable sections of the society, who are likely to suffer disproportionately more than others.

Agile Execution Plan

The approved projects are like corporate firefighting and most of us are great at it. So, I will not dwell too much on that. Bring on a leader, identify the execution team together, and execute. Diversity of skills and experience is valuable in the team. If you have a former emergency room nurse or a former special forces individual, please include them on the team. They may turn out to be the most valuable player here.

Monitor progress and be agile because the context will evolve.

The various steps will likely include some research to verify assumptions and validate the approach, secure resources, and make the project execution effective. There may not be enough time for detailed planning, so tangible intermediate milestones will help. The gated approach is appropriate with clearly defined decision authority. It is now standard project management with significant schedule pressure.

Whether you come out positive or negative will depend on leadership agility, organization's capacity to innovate, and of course financial reserves to live through the tough time.

Control Station

It is always helpful to have a central control station to manage your projects in a Tough Time. You need to look at the pros and cons of having something physical, virtual, or mobile depending upon the seriousness and the duration of the activity.

Lessons Learned

Once you go through this exercise, you would know enough to build a resiliency plan, and handle it the next time; just like our body builds immunity to the virus after it is eradicated.

Example – The Tough Time from the Pandemic

March 2020: Within a couple of weeks, all of us were kicked '*Out of the Box,*' by the Coronavirus. Even though we had some early warning in the US, we stayed complacent as it was on the other side of the planet, forgetting that the *World is* already *Flat.*

In the coming months, significant new content will be created on the Coronavirus pandemic, providing insights into medical science, pharma industry, technical solutions, human considerations, political agendas, social support, industrial impacts, media influence, environmental benefits, and even conspiracy theories. Valuable contributions are already coming from scholars and consulting firms. My interpretation of the situation has been a very humbling experience, looking at it from an Innovation Value Chain perspective as discussed in this chapter.

Rapid Situation Analysis

Preliminary objective: For most organizations the first thing was to protect the employees and citizens from exposure to the virus; then conserve cash and begin exploring ways to maintain operations.

Context: Each individual, company, community, and nation were in a somewhat different situation to resolve: from sick employees, disrupted supply chain, to revenue drops; all requiring different specific solutions. CDC and WHO provided a broad external context useful from employee health perspective. Big Consulting firms were offering guidance and outlook to businesses on their website, as a goodwill gesture. These online resources were good, however, most business owners had to assess their specific situation. Manufacturing, material flow, and people movement and interaction were the major items disrupted by coronavirus. So, in a sense everyone was impacted to varying degrees. The common phrase was "We are all in this together" although the impact varied from favorable to highly adverse. I liked the statement *"We are all in the same storm, but not in the same boat."*

Scenarios: McKinsey defined three scenarios for COVID-19 situation, as (a) quick recovery, (b) global slowdown, and (c) global pandemic/recession. Then more scenarios emerged and were fondly referred by the characteristic shape of economic recovery – U, V, W, or L. By the time you get this book, it would have unfolded into one of these.

We will see multiple ripple effects. The supply chain may be permanently altered with reshoring, in-sourcing, and move away from China. Teleworking might become a very acceptable norm across many industries. There may be excess hospital capacity in various parts of the word. The faith in artificial intelligence and digitalization may reach whole new levels. Government funding might have a permanent shift in priorities. FDA, CDC, and WHO might get an overhaul, and so on. Virtually every sector will have a major change. Even the medical devices and pharma industries that are enjoying the limelight today may need to reevaluate their purposes.

Leadership Charter: This took the form: 'Protect employees and re-establish ways to minimize disruption in customer deliveries.' For those whose purpose was aligned with the need of the day had objectives like, 'Triple the production of hand sanitizers and face masks, within a week'. When some stability in new cases, think about reopening and safely restarting, in search of a new normal.

Those driven by purely financial purpose got into price gouging and hoarding of hand sanitizer and face masks. So unfortunate.

Open Ideation

Solicited and unsolicited ideas were sought and thrown around freely in social media. Even DoD and NSF came out with fast track Small Business Innovation Research solicitation on medical and non-medical solutions. Maker spaces were buzzing with activity. I had the importance of Open-source Innovation reinforced.

During the pandemic, working from home, we developed virtual ideation techniques, which up until then I did not think were possible.

Quick Concept Qualification

The canvas proposed in this chapter emerged out of the crisis and had not seen a full up application, at the time of publication. Although we did apply pieces of it with multiple clients through virtual meetings. Each organization used their existing concept qualification (business case or feasibility analysis) to the best of their ability – in the spirit of crisis, and absence of readiness.

Agile Execution

We had amazing examples of agile execution all across. Beer breweries transformed into hand sanitizer manufacturing with days. Personal protective equipment, hospital beds, ventilators, masks, and other supporting items got into the manufacturing and supply chain very quickly. Multiple designs came out demonstrating frugal and Eco-adaptive Innovation.

Within 2 months, we saw almost every type of innovation discussed so far.

Outlook

As of June 2020, most folks are awaiting a new normal. Numerous discussions amongst thought leaders are bringing out possibilities. For those looking for business opportunities from the pandemic find plenty in pushing Industry 4.0 or digital transformation across all sectors for social good. Robotics, automation, drones, artificial intelligence, telemedicine, augmented reality will be on the rise at most workplaces and homes. Education, healthcare, public sector, communications, and sustainability solutions will be on an upswing, while insurance, airlines, and retail will see a prolonged tough time. Transportation, entertainment, and manufacturing will transform into a new normal, a little difficult to predict.

Challenges include finding new ways to build trust when personal contact and travel is restricted. During the transition, how do you capture market insight, when most of your customer are also equally uncertain.

Let's Summarize

Tough times require Burst Innovation characterized by clearly defined specific objectives, open ideation, simple yet robust qualification, and agile execution. Depending upon the complexity of your situation and context, the Burst Innovation event could be a few hours to a few days and will most likely generate some outrageous solutions. Some of them will require leadership from the gut, rather than data.

Remember you are out-of-the-box. A good possibility is that the box got moved, crushed, deformed, or reformed. You may need to find a new box, or a path into the reformed box. You won't find that with the same style that allowed you to play well within the original box. So please embrace the new situation, requiring a new line of thinking, and let us accept that for a while, it will be an **innovators time to lead**.

Let's Take a Selfie

Our adjustment to the pandemic was?

☐ Very Difficult, because _____

☐ Difficult, because _____

☐ Easy, because _____

Our biggest struggle/pain/fear in early days was (Mark with 'x')

☐ Understand the situation.
☐ Sort out misinformation and noise.
☐ Search for policies and procedures to implement.
☐ Stay in compliance with internal and government requirements.
☐ Deal with employee emotional fallout.
☐ Deal with sick employees.
☐ Establish work from home protocol.
☐ Understand customer, who was also facing the same uncertainty.
☐ Conserve cash flow.
☐ … and …
☐

Our primary challenge during recovery included (Mark with 'x')

☐ Generating and preparing for scenarios that we may face.
☐ Defining a clear set of objectives.
☐ Generating ideas to resolve issues.
☐ Finding resources to resolve issues.
☐ Building trust in the marketplace.
☐ Explore and test options and opportunities.
☐ … and …
☐

8.   *Time to Reflect*

CELEBRATE WHAT YOU'VE ACCOMPLISHED,
BUT RAISE THE BAR A LITTLE HIGHER EACH TIME YOU SUCCEED
– MIA HAMM

During early years my innovation journey was a series of hits and trials. Then I came to corporate America, and was thrust into the world of process control, typically the lean six sigma type. I could see the value and the downside. The entire motivation to start my coaching practice was to blend the concepts of structured process with creativity in a manner that makes innovation affordable, with managed risk. That led to the creation of the simple **Innovation Value Chain** discussed here; which has now been applied at over a dozen clients. Most of the time people understand the individual pieces, however, the real joy becomes visible on their faces when they go through this from a blank piece of paper to the launch of a project.

Introspection

My company/department gains customer insight through ...

I personally gather customer insight through ...

My department performs competitive assessment though …

I personally gather competitive intelligence from …

We generate novel ideas using …

We progressively explore the feasibility of new ideas using

Our team handles failures at attempting something new by ...

We benchmarked our project management process in year 20___ against

If I suddenly get 10 times more budget for innovation projects to invest, with no requirement for returns, I would do the following ...

If I were the top leader or owner of this organization, I would change the following ...

My Going Forward Action Plan

I Commit to

- ☐ ..
- ☐ ..
- ☐ ..
- ☐ ..
- ☐ ..

I Promise to

- ☐ ..
- ☐ ..
- ☐ ..
- ☐ ..
- ☐ ..

Visit us online at http://www.InspiringNext.com/Books/Selfie for an analytical self-assessment, and an opportunity for the latest content on the topic.

What Next?

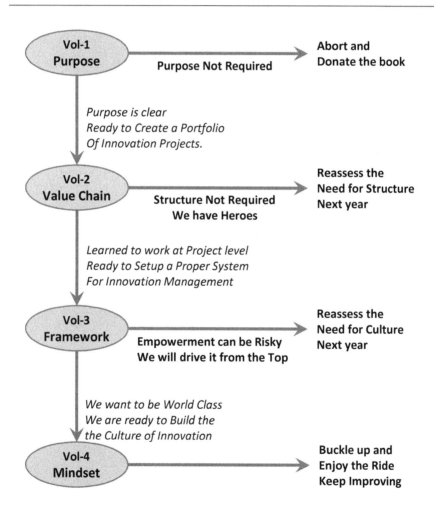

Summary[50] of Volume-3
Inspiring Next Innovation Framework

You Don't Have To Be A Genius Or A Visionary Or A Graduate,
You Just Need A Framework And A Dream – Michael Dell

For years, people have been made to believe that innovation is a privilege of the gifted few. Well, the gifted folks do it naturally, and for the rest of us, it comes with training, ambiance, and some method to the madness. In my early days of innovation coaching practice, I had a matrix of exactly 25 processes and tools to *Enable organizations to build a culture of Robust Innovation and Productivity Improvement* (my original mission statement in 2014). Like many entrepreneurs, I had ventured into the market with little market insight and some appreciation of the innovation value chain. At one of the conferences, I bumped into a former colleague Dr. Gopi Katragadda, who had just taken over as Chief Technology Officer for the Tata Group, a $110 billion conglomerate. He asked, if I could help him use my toolset for his 90 business units that span from Tea to Automobiles. My quick response was *"I am a butterfly; I should not go out on a date with an elephant."* He laughed out loud and probably thought '*What if the elephant wants to go on a date with the butterfly.*' He still left me with an open-ended offer to get back to him if and when I think I was ready. Although I was convinced that they should work with McKinsey or Accenture and not Ripi Singh, I got into looking at redefining the matrix, to drive consistency and confidence across diverse business units of a global entity. The +4π **Innovation Framework** was born, for use by any organization. I got back to the Tata group, but it was too late. By then, that elephant had gone on a

---

date with a bumblebee. You see, the beauty in engaging with leaders like Gopi, is they leave you with inspiring questions and confidence that even a butterfly can date an elephant. Their early feedback validated the Framework application.

Coming back to the evolution of innovation; for the last three centuries, we have seen many entrepreneurs convert their inventions to products of value and change the lifestyle. Nowadays, innovative products are a result of multidisciplinary engagement, and entrepreneurship requires serious business and marketing skills. Large corporations struggle to innovate faster, cheaper, better. So many books hit the market on the topic, each addressing some elements of value. Still, the leaders struggle. The books provide the ingredients; you need a recipe that helps create a dish to your taste. Where does that come from?

On one side, the business schools will teach you the need for vision, objectives, planning, IP management, knowledge augmentation, strategy, etc., and they all appear to be jumbled up in real life. Management Professors and consultants tout that their tools and approach is the best one, because they believe in them, just like me. On the other hand, every organization leader, chartered to innovate, is driven by his/her competencies and management objectives; essentially their taste preference. That creates a real challenge - *'How to manage innovation for excellence in outcome?*

The +4π Innovation Framework Layout

The Framework described in Volume-3 addresses the need. It is a structured matrix of five *Innovation Profiles* and four synergistic *Activity Tracks*, as laid out in the graphic below. It provides a structure to the application of various tools and processes. Enterprise-level excellence emerges through synergy, continuity, and connectivity of the best practices; use of the same language, measures, and monitoring. This holistic approach is often missing in organizations despite their focus on process optimization.

Tracks ↓ / Profile →	Aware	Agile Follower	Smart Forecaster	Visionary Trendsetter	Robust & Resilient
Innovation Strategy	Investment Focus; The Revolution(s); Self Identity; Maps and Gaps; Transition Journey	□ Purpose Definition; □ Charter Definition; □ Success Dashboard; □ Industry 4.0 Impact; □ Innovation Roadmap; □ Competitive Benchmarking; □ Customer Insight	□ Competitive Intelligence; □ Evolutionary Innovation; □ Industry 4.0 Opportunity; □ Society 5.0 Opportunity; □ Customer Shared Vision; □ Portfolio Management	□ Trendsetting Innovation; □ New Line Qualification; □ Customer Shared Values; □ Peripheral Vision; □ Sustainable Planet	□ Disruptive Innovation; □ Disruption Resiliency; □ Thought Map; □ Scenario Planning
Innovation Capital	Expertise Logic; Innovation Mindset; Maps and Gaps	□ Expertise Mapping; □ Expertise Planning; □ Talent Development	□ Dual Career Path; □ Knowledge Management; □ Asset Management; □ Team Development; □ Leadership 4.0; □ Expertise for Industry 4.0	□ Capital Supplements; □ Organization Development	□ Succession Planning; □ Network of Excellence
Innovative Activity	The Value Chain; Maps and Gaps	□ DRIVE: not DMAIC or PDCA; □ Ideation Techniques; □ Frugal Innovation; □ IP Strategy; □ ISO 56000 Awareness	□ Hackathon / Dolphin Tank; □ Concept Qualification; □ Phase-Gate Process; □ Risk Management; □ Burst Innovation; □ ISO 56000 Conformance	□ Open Innovation; □ Biz Model Innovation; □ Peripheral Innovation; □ Crisis Innovation; □ Bold Innovation	
Lean Innovation	Process Integration; Entities Alignment; Maps and Gaps	□ Value Stream Integrity; □ Internal Objective Alignment; □ External Market Alignment; □ Innovation Club; □ Employee Recognition; □ Customer Feedback Loop	□ Customer Mapping; □ Innovation Summit; □ Growth Alignment; □ Incident Management; □ Enterprise Software		

Profile

Culture of Innovation

Inspiring NEXT
Purposeful Innovation

The Five Innovation Profiles

The innovation profiles as defined earlier in chapter-1, are

1. *Aware:* Have successfully innovated and **know** how to.
2. *Agile Follower:* Innovate profitably in **response** to market demand.
3. *Smart Forecaster:* Innovate in **anticipation** of market demand.
4. *Visionary Trendsetter:* Innovate and **create** a market demand.
5. *Robust & Resilient:* Visionary Trendsetters **immune** to market changes.

This definition is simplistic. It helps create a starting point, but you need a bit more to self-assess and a lot more to improve your profile. Over the years, many more characteristics have emerged that define the profile and organization behavior, or culture, or attitude towards innovation. These are all discussed in detail throughout the Volume-3.

The Four Activity Tracks

The synergistic activity tracks are

1. *Innovation Strategy* provides direction.
2. *Innovation Capital* addresses resources.
3. *Innovative Activity* is for effective execution.
4. *Lean Innovation* makes it efficient.

Volume-3 Chapter-1 defines the $+4\pi$ Innovation Framework model along with several profile characteristics. It also compares the proposed Framework with some of the well-established models from McKinsey, Booz & Company, Boston Consulting Group, as well as ISO. Most of them seem to either discuss outcomes (equivalent to profiles) or efforts (equivalent to tracks). The $+4\pi$ Framework is the only one with a full matrix style, making it easier to use as an actionable set of tools.

The Framework Design

Let us look at the framework, one track at a time, and see how various tools buildup the profile.

Track - Innovation Strategy

This track defines the strategic roadmap – the products and services a company would develop along with a timeline to capture the market share. Most of us have some form of a roadmap. It may be a simple list of things to do in a sequence; or a full up graphic representation of projects linked to markets and resources along with timelines. The important things are the quality of data used to create the roadmap, how far ahead are you looking, and how much uncertainty you are prepared to handle. All these are explicitly connected with and determine your innovation profile.

Volume-3 Chapter-2 provides an overview of tools and methods to understand the marketplace for building a strategic innovation roadmap. The set of tools in this track progressively adds rigor to the roadmap through deeper customer insight, competitive intelligence, technology trends and forecasting, investment management, and uncertainty management.

A strategic roadmap is like the GPS for your car that guides you through the fastest or shortest route to your destination.

Track - Innovation Capital

This track includes developing and managing critical resources to support the Innovation Strategy and build a competitive advantage in today's knowledge economy. Most us think in terms of funding as a primary resource, the 'Cash is King' philosophy. Today, 'Talent is King' and the 'Cash is Queen.' Talents and its ability to create new knowledge, apply existing knowhow, secure IP is a differentiator. The approach to capital development is also profile dependent.

Volume-3 Chapter-3 provides tools and processes to progressively develop the innovation capital to build a sustainable organization, have strong partnerships, and even support a healthy ecosystem. Set of tools guide subject matter expertise & leadership development, high-performance team building, knowledge augmentation, leveraging networks, succession planning; all using novel visual maps.

Innovation capital is like the power under the hood of your car that will enable you to reach your destination.

Track - Innovative Activity

This track defines the process to systematically develop new products, reducing risk and cost. This guides the team through an innovation value chain which begins with a white space or a market demand, and ends with an emotionally engaged customer.

Volume-3 Chapter-4, puts it all in context of Innovation Profiles.

Innovation activity is like traveling in your car.

Track - Lean Innovation

This track aligns products, processes, employees, customers, and business metrics, to continuously improve the efficiency and productivity of the innovation. Most of us have lean initiatives and they often stifle creativity. This track is designed to work specifically with the three tracks above to remain creative.

Volume-3 Chapter-5 provides guidance to assure effectiveness and efficiency through (a) continuity of processes (b) alignment with customers and markets, (c) alignment across roadmap, employees, and suppliers, and (d) cloud-based information management platform, based on the Framework. These things all help reduce the execution friction. This set of tools guides the employee morale and customer engagement from management objectives, providing synergistic benefits making the whole greater than the sum of individual pieces.

This is like the 4-wheel alignment and balancing to run the car smoothly without serious tire wear and fuel inefficiency.

Framework Application

If you look closely you would notice the 3rd track – *Innovative Activity* only goes up to *Trendsetter* profile. This is so because to become *Robust and Resilient* you only need a strong strategy and capital. On similar lines, the 4th track of *Lean Innovation* only goes up to *Forecaster*. The premise being, you need to get all your processes aligned and effective by the time you become a Forecaster and shouldn't be thinking of efficiencies from alignment while being a *Trendsetter*.

According to this Framework, if your company can reach the level of *Smart Forecaster* you can claim to have built a culture of innovation. This may be a good position for many; because the risk goes up sharply as you move to be a *Trendsetter,* and everyone does not need to get there.

If you do a quick self-check, you will likely discover that you do not necessarily belong to one vertical column. Most of the companies are like that. Also, you may not be consistent in your behavior to stay in one column all the time. That is a good thing. It goes to show your capability, which is always higher than typical performance; and gaps across various rows where you need to change to move the profile. Once you figure out your current innovation profile and your desired state, Volume-3 will help you build the processes and prepare you for Volume-4 to reset the mindset.

This Framework is continuously evolving; you can get the latest copy by reaching out to the author.

Framework in a Tough Time

Volume-3 Chapter-6 briefly discusses the value of the Framework in a tough time and how it can be adapted in a crisis.

Let's Summarize

An organization's ability to innovate is a key factor for sustained growth, economic viability, increased well-being, and the development of society. An innovation management system guides the organization from the purpose to valuable intended outcomes through proper use of tools, processes, best practices, and development of an innovation mindset.

The $+4\pi$ Innovation Framework is designed to empower leaders with a holistic view of innovation management – purposeful and sustainable.

Let's Take a Selfie

I can see some of these symptoms in my organization …

- ☐ Developing products in response to market need (or RFP).
- ☐ Always competing on cost.
- ☐ Market share is declining.
- ☐ Business is stable, yet stagnant.
- ☐ Projects are running late or over budget, or missing expectations.
- ☐ Quality is being compromised to be profitable.
- ☐ Customer complaints are increasing.
- ☐ Top talent is walking out.
- ☐ … any more alarms …
- ☐

I am familiar with the following innovation management models …

- ☐ McKinsey's – 3 horizons.
- ☐ Booz & Co – 3 strategies.
- ☐ Boston Consulting Group – 6 types.
- ☐ Johns Hopkins Applied Physics Laboratory.
- ☐ Innovation 360.
- ☐ … others such as …
- ☐

Action: Please go back 6 pages to the Framework graphic and 'x' mark the processes you need to improve or create afresh. List your top 3 here …

- ☐

- ☐

- ☐

Summary[51] of Volume-4
Inspiring Next Innovation Mindset

THE INNOVATION KILLERS ARE ALMOST ALWAYS NEATLY
DISGUISED AS PROTECTORS OF THE ORGANIZATION.
– THOMAS KOULOPOULOS?

As a coach, I once worked for a company that had been highly focused on operations for a long time, with innovation being sidelined even in the engineering department. I was a little surprised. Is it possible to have a large number of engineers and yet no innovation in the department? Deeper discovery revealed that several creative types were doing high-tech projects in their basement or at local incubator on stuff completely unrelated to their job; no conflict of interest; nothing illegal; they just needed to flex their innovation muscle. But why couldn't they do it at the workplace that may even have a business need for them to do so? My contract did not last long.

By now, I have probably heard every excuse why companies are not able to innovate. Every time, I hear a very genuine concern or a legitimate reason, the above quote rings in my ear. Innovation appears to be a priority, yet even the successful leadership struggles to innovate consistently. Are they trapped in the very system that they created to help them grow?[52]. Some companies have added the word **'innovation'** to their mission, vision, or value statements **without making it clear** to the organization what exactly it means to them. They need a program and an action plan, to follow through.

---

[51] You may skip it, if you plan to read the Volume-4.
[52] The Innovators' Dilemma; Clayton M. Christensen; Book; May 2002.

Struggle to Innovate

There are several reasons holding executives back from taking steps to create innovation-driven differentiation to change their destiny. Some highly visible aspects include leadership mindset – quarter to quarter performance, incentives, risk-averse style, too much familiarity with the market, etc.

Then there are the human minds at play, which are statistically distributed and only about 16% are innovators or early adapters. The organizations show a basic physical phenomenon:

- **Friction**: Opposing force resisting relative motion.
- **Inertia**: Tendency to do nothing or to remain unchanged.
- **Energy**: The capacity for doing work.
- **Momentum**: Impetus gained by a moving object.

Volume-4 Chapter-2 discusses how to overcome inertia/friction and build momentum through these four steps.

Your Next Mindset Step

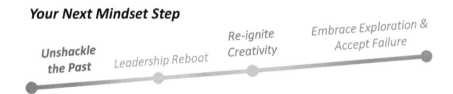

Unshackle the Past

Initiatives such as six-sigma which add value to repeatable activities such as manufacturing, are not particularly suited for new product development. Lean helps with productivity, and perhaps innovation at the process level, not so much at ideation for content or creative outcomes.

Volume-4 Chapter-3 questions various aspects of traditional management and some popular business bestsellers, that are akin to dead weight on the feet.

> When people say, innovation is unaffordable;
> I ask *"Do you know the cost of not innovating?*

Reboot Leadership

According to Linda Hill[53], innovation leadership is about creating a space, where people are willing and able to work hard, share, and combine talent and passion to innovatively solve a problem. Some of the characteristics include

- They are open to rapid continuous change.
- They are open-minded and willing to take risks.
- They usually take this customer-first perspective.
- They embrace the iterative nature of Innovation.
- They align innovation strategy with overall business purpose.
- They stay out of the way of people innovating.
- They defer judgment, focus on success criteria.
- They accept failure, even on unapproved tasks.
- They build communities that enjoy experiments.

Leaders understand that ultimately, innovation is more about mindset than skill set. They are not fooled into thinking that innovation is easy. They are prepared to roll up their sleeves.

Peter Drucker says, *"In innovation, there is talent, there is ingenuity, and there is knowledge. But when it is said and done, what innovation requires is hard, focused, purposeful work."*

Volume-4 Chapter-4 covers various aspects of leadership – mind, style, attitude, gender, and a C-level role – The Chief Innovation Officer.

---

[53] How to Manage for Collective Creativity; Linda Hill; Ted Talk, March 13, 2015;
https://www.ted.com/talks/linda_hill_how_to_manage_for_collective_creativity?language=tlh.

Re-ignite Creativity

If we agree that innovation is a mental muscle, then we accept that it needs a daily workout. And periodic health check. Or as Simon Sinek says, dental hygiene requires daily brushing of the teeth as well as a bi-annual cleaning to keep them healthy. To re-ignite creativity across the organization, you need to make a conscious effort on several activities that over some time can build the mental muscle, such as …

- Inspiring everyday language.
- Weekly innovation minute in staff meetings.
- Quarterly Dolphin Tank type open ideation competition.
- Annual Innovation Summit or open day to showcase.
- Couple of hackathons.
- Gamify innovation.

Hiring an innovator is trickier than we think. A typical hiring process, which is designed to quickly eliminate potential low performers, also ends up identifying an innovator as a misfit. Promoting an innovator comes with a challenge on people skills and might require a dual career path for retention.

Volume-4 Chapter-5 covers all of these in simple executable steps.

Embrace Exploration and Accept Failures

We can make a conscious effort to learn by strategically producing failures, through systematic experimentation[54]. Researchers in basic science know that a large percentage of experiments will fail. First, they know that failure is not optional in their work; it is a part of being at the leading edge of scientific discovery. Second, far more than most of us, they understand

---

[54] Strategies for Learning from Failure; Amy Edmondson; HBR; https://hbr.org/2011/04/strategies-for-learning-from-failure; April 2011.

that every failure conveys valuable information, and they are eager to get it before the competition does.

On the other side, the corporate managers, vary of failure, typically do whatever they can to make sure that the test is perfect right out from the start. They design optimal conditions rather than representative ones, leading to a successful demonstration and a failed project later. That's why I am very concerned when my clients boast of the success rate in their product review process.

Exceptional organizations are those that go beyond detecting and analyzing failures and try to generate intelligent ones for the express purpose of learning and innovating. It is not that managers in these organizations enjoy failure. But they recognize it as a necessary by-product of experimentation. They also realize that they do not have to do big experiments with large budgets. Often a small pilot, a dry run of a new technique, or a simulation will suffice.

The courage to confront our own and others' imperfections is crucial to solving the apparent contradiction of wanting neither to discourage the reporting of problems, nor to create an environment in which anything is acceptable. This means that managers must ask employees to be brave and speak up—and must not respond by expressing anger or strong disapproval of what may at first appear to be incompetence. More often than we realize, complex systems are at work behind organizational failures, and their lessons and improvement opportunities are lost when the conversation is stifled.

Failures are a significant contributor to building a strong character, confidence, and a believable personality. I have a difficult time working with those, who claim they have never failed. Either the claim is false, or the explorer in them is non-existent. In addition to Subject Matter Learning, failure breaks down our egos, and promotes team bonding and integrity.

Volume-4 Chapter-6 discusses these aspects at length and demonstrates those with case-studies from some very successful corporations, such as Google and Apple.

Mindset in a Tough Time

Volume-4 Chapter-7 briefly discusses the innovation mindset in a tough time and how it is helping humanity with the pandemic situation at the time of writing this book in mid-2020.

Time to Liberate

Volume-4 Chapters-9-11 are planning exercises to identify your future state, and a pathway to get there, based on all the selfie moments throughout the four volumes.

Let's Summarize

Building an innovation mindset is the key to sustained innovative activity, in normal times as well as tough times. It takes numerous activities, language, commitment, consistency, over a long period and the progress is invisible for the most part, until one day, you just feel very different. It is just like you keep dating for a while and one day you suddenly feel you are in love.

This building of a mental muscle requires to break away from the past, and stick to the exercise routine with patience.

Let's Take a Selfie

 # I think the following reasons are holding us back from innovating …

- ☐ We believe that our customers are not ready for this.
- ☐ To the best of our knowledge, our primary competitors are not doing it.
- ☐ We do not have energy to deal with regulatory bodies.
- ☐ We have had desired growth for so many years; why disturb it now.
- ☐ We are already very innovative.
- ☐ Our management consultant thinks it is too risky.
- ☐ There is no proven formula to innovate, that works all the time.
- ☐ … any more
- ☐ …

 # I think the right questions to ask are …

- ☐ How much should I spend on innovation?
- ☐ How much should I invest in Innovation?
- ☐ How much will it cost me if I choose not to innovate?
- ☐ … any more
- ☐ …

 # We have the following innovation leadership roles in our Company

- ☐ Chief Innovation Officer.
- ☐ Chief Engineer/Architect/Scientist/Artist/Actuary/….
- ☐ Chief of Talent, or Knowledge Chief, or Delivery Chief.
- ☐ Customer Experience Chief.
- ☐ Chief of Products and Services.
- ☐ … any more
- ☐ …

We have the following in our organization …

☐ A designated space, free to capture and play around with ideas.
☐ A campaign to discourage the use of certain common language.
☐ Conversation around innovations in other industries in staff meetings.
☐ Ideation or hackathon type competitive events.
☐ Annual meeting around innovation with senior staff.
☐ Sponsorship of innovation events outside of the company.
☐   … any more
☐   …

I can accept a failure in …

☐ Process deviation – Deliberate.
☐ Process deviation – Unintentional.
☐ Lack of ability.
☐ Process inadequacy.
☐ Challenging task.
☐ Process complexity.
☐ Dealing with uncertainty.
☐ Hypothesis testing.
☐ Exploratory study.
☐   … any more
☐   …
☐
☐

Appendix – Perceptions Unfolded

---

*A LOT OF WHAT WE SAY BEFORE A REVOLUTION IS
WRONG AFTER THE FACT. – RIPI SINGH*

The predictions from proven leaders of their time, in their domain of excellence, have turned out to be incorrect. There are many reasons for that.

- We have biases anchored around our experience.
- It is easier to spot quick changes as compared to gradual ones.
- We are poor at understanding the confluence of multiple factors changing at the same time.
- We are poor at predicting changing human needs and response to breakthroughs.

> If companies like Google and Apple can have their share of failed projects, leaders can have their share of failed predictions.

Here are some interesting historic quotes from leaders of the industry that I have compiled from various sources on the internet, and would like to share with a humbling perspective that how difficult it can be to predict, rather than being judgmental.

Through the 1st Industrial Revolution

(1800s) How, sir, would you make a ship sail against the wind and currents by lighting a bonfire under her deck? I pray you, excuse me, I have not the time to listen to such nonsense. — Napoleon Bonaparte.

(1830) Rail travel at high speed is not possible because passengers, unable to breathe, would die of asphyxia. — Dr. Dionysius Lardner.

(1864) No one will pay good money to get from Berlin to Potsdam in one hour when he can ride his horse there in one day for free. — King William I of Prussia.

Through the 2ⁿᵈ Industrial Revolution

(1876) The Americans may need the telephone, but we do not. We have plenty of messenger boys. — William Preece, British Post Office.

(1876) This 'telephone' has too many shortcomings to be seriously considered as a means of communication. The device is inherently of no value to us. — Western Union.

(1880) Everyone acquainted with the subject will recognize [the light bulb] as a conspicuous failure. — Henry Morton, Stevens Institute of Technology, on Edison's light bulb.

(1889) Fooling around with alternating current (AC) is just a waste of time. Nobody will use it, ever. — Thomas Edison.

(1895) Heavier than air flying machines are impossible. — Lord Kelvin, President of the British Royal Society.

(1901) I must confess that my imagination refuses to see any sort of submarine doing anything but suffocating its crew and floundering at sea. — H.G. Wells, British novelist.

(1903) The horse is here to stay, but the automobile is only a novelty, a fad. — President of Michigan Savings Bank to Henry Ford's lawyers.

(1916) The cinema is a little more than a fad. It's canned drama. What audiences really want to see is flesh and blood on the stage. – Charlie Chaplin.

(1921) The wireless music box has no imaginable commercial value. Who would pay for a message sent to no one in particular? — Associates of David Sarnoff, early radio pioneer.

(1926) Such a man-made voyage [rocket travel] will never occur, regardless of all future endeavors. — Lee DeForest, American inventor.

(1927) Who the hell wants to see actors talk. – H M Warner of Warner Brothers.

(1932) There is not the slightest indication that nuclear energy will ever be obtainable. That would mean that the atom would have to be shattered at will. — Albert Einstein.

(1933) There will never be a bigger plane built. — Boeing engineer, after the first flight of the twin-engine 247 that held 10 people.

(1936) A rocket will never be able to leave the Earth's atmosphere. — New York Times. The Times published a correction in 1969.

(1946) Television won't last, because people will soon get tired of staring at a plywood box every night. — Darryl Zanuck, 20th Century Fox.

(1955) It'll be gone by June. — Variety Magazine, on rock-and-roll.

(1955) Nuclear powered vacuum cleaners will probably be a reality within 10 years. — Alex Lewyt, President of the Lewyt Vacuum Cleaner Company.

(1959) The world potential market for copying machines is 5,000 at most — Executive at IBM to the founders of Xerox.

(1961) There is practically no chance communications space satellites will be used to provide better telephone, telegraph, television or radio service inside the United States. — T.A.M. Craven, FCC commissioner.

(1962) We don't like their sound, and guitar music is on the way out. — Decca Recording Company on declining to sign the Beatles.

(1968) The Japanese auto industry isn't likely to carve out a big slice of the US market. — BusinessWeek magazine.

Through the 3rd Industrial Revolution

(1943) I think there is a world market for maybe five computers. — Thomas Watson, Chairman of IBM.

(1977) There is no reason for any individual to have a computer in his home. — Ken Olson, president of Digital Equipment Corp.

(1968) Remote shopping, while entirely feasible, will flop — Time magazine.

(1995) I predict the internet will soon go spectacularly supernova and in 1996 collapse. — Robert Metcalfe, Founder of 3Com.

(1995) The truth is no online database will replace your daily newspaper. – Cliff Stoll. Newsweek article titled The internet? Bah!

(2003) These Google guys want to be billionaires and rock stars and go to conferences and all that. Let's see if they still want to run the business. in two to three years. — Bill Gates, Chairman of Microsoft.

(2005) There's just not that many videos I want to watch. — Steve Chen, co-founder of YouTube, upon selling his own company to Google.

(2007) There's no chance that the iPhone is going to get any significant market share. No chance. – Steve Ballmer, Microsoft CEO.

Through the 4th Industrial Revolution

(2014) Once unfriendly superintelligence exists, it would prevent us from replacing it or changing its preferences. Our fate would be sealed. … A badly designed AI system will be impossible to correct once deployed – Nick Bostrom in his book Superintelligence.

(2018) I do think we need to be very careful about the advancement of AI. As AI gets probably much smarter than humans, the relative intelligence ratio is probably similar to that between a person and a cat, maybe bigger. – Elon Musk.

(2019) It's impossible that humans could be controlled by machines. They're machines that are invented by humans. - Jack Ma, Alibaba founder.

One of these two (Jack Ma and Elon Musk) will be wrong by 2050.

(2010s) The aerospace industry will never accept 3D printed parts – Various executives and thought leaders.

(2014) 3D printer drones will take to skies by 2040. - BAE scientists.

(2015) Human colony on Mars by 2039. – Buzz Aldrin.

(2018) We will have 1 Trillion humans in the solar system. – Jeff Bezos.

(2019) We will go to a 4-day workweek by 2030, and 3-day by 2040. – Ripi Singh.

(2020) Readers prediction

Appendix – Innovation Standards

GREAT THINGS HAPPEN WHEN THE WORLD AGREES - *ISO*

International Standard: ISO 56000

> According to ISO 56000, "An organization's ability to innovate is recognized as a key factor for sustained growth, economic viability, increased wellbeing, and the development of society. The innovation capability of an organization includes the ability to understand and respond to changing conditions of its context, to pursue new opportunities, and to leverage the knowledge and creativity of people within the organization, and in collaboration with external interested parties."

Evolution of ISO 56000

The scope of ISO-TC/279 is *"Standardization of terminology, tools, methods, and interactions between relevant parties to enable innovation."* The first plenary meeting of ISO-TC/279 was held in Paris in Dec 2013. Since then, it has been meeting twice a year with a focus on a set of standards structured for ease of application.

Standards published will be ISO 56000 series (formerly 50500). These standards on innovation management bring best practices from around the world primarily as a guidance in innovation management. They are written with an intent to define the terminology, facilitate collaboration, develop the tools capability to innovate, manage a host of intricacies, and bring innovations successfully to market. Some of these standards will follow a high-level structure (HLS) which is (0) Introduction, (1) Scope, (2) Normative References, (3) Terms and Definitions, (4) Context of the Organization, (5) Leadership, (6) Planning, (7) Support, (8) Operation, (9) Performance Evaluation, and (10) Improvement.

List of ISO Guidance Documents on Innovation

As of the most recent ISO meeting in May 2020, the list of innovation guidance documents includes the following.

ISO **56000**:2020 Fundamentals and Vocabulary
ISO **56001** Reserved for auditable (certifiable) standard in the future
ISO **56002**:2019 Innovation Management System
ISO **56003**:2019 Tools and Methods for Innovation Partnership
ISO/TR **56004**:2019 Innovation Management Assessment
ISO **56005** Intellectual Property Management (Due Fall 2020)
ISO **56006** Strategic Intelligence Management (Due Winter 2021)
ISO **56007** Idea Management (Due Spring 2022)
ISO **56008** Innovation Operation Measurements/Metrics (Due 2023)
ISO **56010** Illustrative Examples of ISO 56000 (too new to even put a date)

Some of these have already accounted for a 6-12 months extension due to Coronavirus.

Other National Standards on Innovation

TC/279 identified exiting innovation management standards in 2013.

Brazilian Standard

ABNT NBR 16501:2011 - Guidelines for Management Systems R&D+I

British Standard

7000-1:2008 Design management systems. Guide to managing innovation

Chinese Set of Standards

GB/T 29490:2013 Enterprise IP management
GB/T 33250:2016 IP Management for R&D organizations
GB/T 33251:2016 IP Management for higher education institutions

European Set of Standards: Innovation Management (2008)

EN 16555- part 1 – Innovation management system
EN 16555- part 2 – Strategic intelligence management
EN 16555- part 3 – Innovation thinking
EN 16555- part 4 – Intellectual property management
EN 16555- part 5 – Collaborative management
EN 16555- part 6 – Creativity management
EN 16555- part 7 – Innovation management assessment

French Set of Standards

FD X50-146: Innovation Management – IP Management (2010)
FD X50-274: Innovation Management – Creativity management (2015)
FD X50-273: Sustainable development in the innovation process (2014)
FD X50-272: Guidelines for Open Innovation implementation (2014)

German Standard

DIN 77100:2001 – Monetary patent portfolio valuation

Irish Standard

NWA-1:2009 describing activities from strategy to market

Mexican Standard

NMX GT 003:2008 simple pattern for a process management technology

Portuguese Standard

NP4457:2007, Management system requirements of R&D+I

Spanish Standard

UNE 166002 - R&D+I: Requirements Management RD. (2006)

About the Author

Dr. Ripi Singh, is an innovation coach with 3 years of experience and 30 years of learning in product, process, and people leadership; spanning aerospace & defense, renewable energy & power, advanced manufacturing, healthcare and medical devices, IT, and the art of learning itself. His coaching practice has a purpose – Industry 4.0 for Sustainability.

Ripi helps his clients bring affordable innovation into their culture using a holistic approach described in these books. His service spans across mentoring young minds to coaching business owners; startups to growth companies; commodities like garments to futuristic technologies like drones. He engages in global projects in Germany, India, Singapore, China, and the United States. He supports local ecosystem development through collaborative innovation spaces in State of Connecticut. People jokingly call him Ripi 4.0.

Ripi 3.0 served the corporate world as Director R&D Alstom Power (now General Electric), as Advanced Technology Manager for United Technologies, and as Chief Engineer at Karta Technologies. During those 16 years, he successfully delivered advanced technologies on high impact and leading-edge aviation and energy programs. He also performed foundational research on aviation system sustainment and life extensions in collaboration with industry and universities.

Ripi 2.0 was an academician, serving in the Faculty of Aerospace Engineering, and supporting aerospace industrial sector in Bangalore India. Over a decade, he did fundamental research in materials fatigue and fracture mechanics necessary for flight safety; and contributed to US Navy and EU projects in the 1990s.

Ripi 1.0 was making working models of earthmoving machinery in middle and high schools for science fairs and exhibitions in India, before he was exposed to a calculator during sophomore engineering.

Ripi has been felicitated with numerous national and corporate honors, authorship of 75+ publications, 250+ lectures, two patents, and other accolades. He has won the *'President of India Cash Prize'* for outstanding research, *'Calcutta Convention Award'* for excellence in Technical Education, *'Tata Fellowship'* for Research; All of these national recognitions qualified him for naturalized US citizenship under the category of *'Outstanding Researcher with Extraordinary Ability.'*

Ripi serves on Technical Committee 279 as US delegate to ISO 56000 on Innovation Management Guidance, Chair of NDE 4.0 for American Society for Non-Destructive Testing, the council of the Connecticut Academy of Science and Engineering, Guest editor for Springer on NDE 4.0, Industrial advisory board for Entrepreneurship and Innovation at University of New Haven, University of Hartford, Tsinghua University, and International Association of Innovation Professionals. He holds a BS, MS, and a Ph.D. in Aerospace Engineering, a post-doc from Georgia Tech, and an Executive MS in Business Strategy from RPI, always with highest GPA.

Ripi's wife Anu Kaur is a cancer research scientist and they have one son Amanjot Singh, a practicing mechanical engineer. Ripi loves music, dance, and photography. His study of different faiths has taken him to Vatican City, Jerusalem City, Salt Lake City, Amritsar, Badrinath, Tirupati, and many other popular religious shrines around the world.

Look out for more titles on Inspiring Next from Ripi Singh

1. Inspiring Next Innovation Purpose
2. Inspiring Next Innovation Value Chain
3. Inspiring Next Innovation Framework
4. Inspiring Next Innovation Mindset
5. Inspiring Next Purposeful Innovation – Text Book
6. Inspiring Next Innovation in Tough Times
7. Inspiring Next Innovations for a Safer World
8. Inspiring Next Innovations in Energy Systems
9. Inspiring Next Enriched Living
10. Inspiring Next Ecosystem Revolution

Just thought of sharing a perspective as we close this volume.

Consultant	Coach
Solves Client's problem	Builds client's competency to solve the problem
Transaction relationship, finite duration, with defined deliverable and closure	Empathic relationship, longer lasting, with no defined end point
Tangible, visible, explicit solution outcome	Intangible, invisible, implicit competency building
Expected to be more competent than the client on the subject of transactions	Expected to make the client more competent than client believes possible on their subject
Protective of his skills, tools and tricks	Shares his skills to develop the client
Vested in the task outcome	Vested in client success
Solution speed controlled by the consultant	Developmental pace controlled by the client
Good for solving a problem	Required to search the right problem

Motivation	Inspiration
External pull to perform & accomplish	Internal drive or urge to pursue
Pulled towards a goal or an objective	Driven towards a purpose
Rewards are generally visible & tangible	Rewards are invisible & intangible
Aligned with management styles	Aligned with leadership attitude
Good for improving productivity	Required to foster innovation

Front Cover: An inventor demonstrates the power of innovation value chain via a prototype of an integrated home health device to his mentor.

CPSIA information can be obtained
at www.ICGtesting.com
Printed in the USA
LVHW051757141020
668674LV00011B/683